CAPITALISM AND FREEDOM

Milton Friedman is a senior research fellow at the Hoover Institution, Stanford University, and the Paul Snowden Russell Distinguished Service Professor Emeritus of Economics at the University of Chicago. In 1976 he was awarded the Nobel Memorial Prize in Economics. With his wife, Rose D. Friedman, he wrote the best-selling book, *Free to Choose* (1980) and a joint memoir (1998).

CAPITALISM AND FREEDOM

40th Anniversary Edition

With a new Preface by the Author

MILTON FRIEDMAN

WITH THE ASSISTANCE OF ROSE D. FRIEDMAN

The University of Chicago Press
Chicago and London

To

Janet and David

and their contemporaries
who must carry the torch of liberty
on its next lap

The University of Chicago Press, Chicago 60637
The University of Chicago Press, Ltd., London
Copyright © 1962, 1982, 2002 by The University of Chicago
All rights reserved. Originally published 1962
Reissued with a new Preface in 1982, and again in 2002.
Printed in the United States of America
18 17 16 15 14 13 12   *10 11 12 13*
ISBN-13: 978-0-226-26420-2 (cloth)
ISBN-13: 978-0-226-26421-9 (paper)
ISBN-10: 0-226-26420-3 (cloth)
ISBN-10: 0-226-26421-1 (paper)

Library of Congress Cataloging-in-Publication Data

Friedman, Milton, 1912–
    Capitalism and freedom / Milton Friedman ; with the assistance
of Rose D. Friedman ; with a new preface by the author—
40th anniversary ed.
        p.   cm.
    Includes bibliographical references and index.
    ISBN 0-226-26420-3 (cloth : alk. paper) — ISBN 0-226-26421-1
(paper : alk. paper)
        1. Capitalism. 2. State, The. 3. Liberty. 4. United States—
Economic policy. I. Friedman, Rose D. II. Title.

HB501 .F7   2002
330.12′2—dc21

                                            2002067530

⊗ The paper used in this publication meets the minimum
requirements of the American National Standard for
Information Sciences—Permanence of Paper for Printed
Library Materials, ANSI Z39.48-1992.

Contents

Preface, 2002

IN MY PREFACE TO THE 1982 edition of this book, I documented a dramatic shift in the climate of opinion, manifested in the difference between the way this book was treated when it was first published in 1962, and the way my wife's and my subsequent book, *Free to Choose,* presenting the same philosophy, was treated when it was published in 1980. That change in the climate of opinion developed while and partly because the role of government was exploding under the influence of initial welfare state and Keynesian views. In 1956, when I gave the lectures that my wife helped shape into this book, government spending in the United States—federal, state, and local—was equal to 26 percent of national income. Most of this spending was on defense. Non-defense spending was 12 percent of national income. Twenty-five years later, when the 1982 edition of this book was published, total spending had risen to 39 percent of national income and non-defense spending had more than doubled, amounting to 31 percent of national income.

That change in the climate of opinion had its effect. It paved the way for the election of Margaret Thatcher in Britain and Ronald Reagan in the United States. They were able to curb Leviathan, though not to cut it down. Total government spending in the United States did decline slightly, from 39 percent of national income in 1982 to 36 percent in 2000, but that was almost all due to a reduction in spending for defense.

Non-defense spending fluctuated around a roughly constant level: 31 percent in 1982, 30 percent in 2000.

The climate of opinion received a further boost in the same direction when the Berlin wall fell in 1989 and the Soviet Union collapsed in 1992. That brought to a dramatic end an experiment of some seventy years between two alternative ways of organizing an economy: top-down versus bottom-up; central planning and control versus private markets; more colloquially, socialism versus capitalism. The result of that experiment had been foreshadowed by a number of similar experiments on a smaller scale: Hong Kong and Taiwan versus mainland China; West Germany versus East Germany; South Korea versus North Korea. But it took the drama of the Berlin Wall and the collapse of the Soviet Union to make it part of conventional wisdom, so that it is now taken for granted that central planning is indeed *The Road to Serfdom,* as Friedrich A. Hayek titled his brilliant 1944 polemic.

What is true for the United States and Great Britain is equally true for the other Western advanced countries. In country after country, the initial postwar decades witnessed exploding socialism, followed by creeping or stagnant socialism. And in all these countries the pressure today is toward giving markets a greater role and government a smaller one. I interpret the situation as reflecting the long lag between opinion and practice. The rapid socialization of the post–World War II decades reflected the prewar shift of opinion toward collectivism; the creeping or stagnant socialism of the past few decades reflects the early effects of the postwar change of opinion; future desocialization will reflect the mature effects of the change in opinion reinforced by the collapse of the Soviet Union.

The change in opinion has had an even more dramatic effect on the formerly underdeveloped world. That has been true even in China, the largest remaining explicitly communist state. The introduction of market reforms by Deng Xiaoping in the late seventies, in effect privatizing agriculture, dramatically increased output and led to the introduction of additional market elements into a communist command society. The limited increase in economic freedom has changed the face of China, strikingly confirming our faith in the power of free markets. China is still very far from being a free society, but there is no doubt that the residents of China are freer and more prosperous than they were under Mao—freer in every dimension except the political. And there are even the first small signs of some increase in political freedom, manifested in the election of some officials in a growing number of villages. China has far to go, but it has been moving in the right direction.

In the immediate post–World War II period, the standard doctrine was that development of the third world required central planning plus massive foreign aid. The failure of that formula wherever it was tried, as was pointed out so effectively by Peter Bauer and others, and the dramatic success of the market-oriented policies of the East Asia tigers—Hong Kong, Singapore, Taiwan, South Korea—has produced a very different doctrine for development. By now, many countries in Latin America and Asia, and even a few in Africa have adopted a market-oriented approach and a smaller role for government. Many of the former Soviet satellites have done the same. In all those cases, in accordance with the theme of this book, increases in economic freedom have gone hand in hand with increases in political and civil freedom and have led to increased prosperity; competitive capitalism and freedom have been inseparable.

A final personal note: It is a rare privilege for an author to be able to evaluate his own work forty years after it first appeared. I appreciate very much having the chance to do so. I am enormously gratified by how well the book has withstood time and how pertinent it remains to today's problems. If there is one major change I would make, it would be to replace the dichotomy of economic freedom and political freedom with the trichotomy of economic freedom, civil freedom, and political freedom. After I finished the book, Hong Kong, before it was returned to China, persuaded me that while economic freedom is a necessary condition for civil and political freedom, political freedom, desirable though it may be, is not a necessary condition for economic and civil freedom. Along these lines, the one major defect in the book seems to me an inadequate treatment of the role of political freedom, which under some circumstances promotes economic and civic freedom, and under others, inhibits economic and civic freedom.

Milton Friedman
Stanford, California
March 11, 2002

Preface, 1982

The lectures that my wife helped shape into this book were delivered a quarter of a century ago. It is hard even for persons who were then active, let alone for the more than half of the current population who were then less than ten years old or had not yet been born, to reconstruct the intellectual climate of the time. Those of us who were deeply concerned about the danger to freedom and prosperity from the growth of government, from the triumph of welfare-state and Keynesian ideas, were a small beleaguered minority regarded as eccentrics by the great majority of our fellow intellectuals.

Even seven years later, when this book was first published, its views were so far out of the mainstream that it was not reviewed by any major national publication—not by the *New York Times* or the *Herald Tribune* (then still being published in New York) or the *Chicago Tribune*, or by *Time* or *Newsweek* or even the *Saturday Review*—though it was reviewed by the London *Economist* and by the major professional journals. And this for a book directed at the general public, written by a professor at a major U.S. university, and destined to sell more than 400,000 copies in the next eighteen years. It is inconceivable that such a publication by an economist of comparable professional standing but favorable to the welfare state or socialism or communism would have received a similar silent treatment.

How much the intellectual climate has changed in the past quarter-century is attested to by the very different reception that greeted my wife's and my book *Free to Choose,* a direct lineal descendant of *Capitalism and Freedom* presenting the same basic philosophy and published in 1980. That book was reviewed by every major publication, frequently in a featured, lengthy review. It was not only partly reprinted in *Book Digest,* but also featured on the cover. *Free to Choose* sold some 400,000 hardcover copies in the U.S. in its first year, has been translated into twelve foreign languages, and was issued in early 1981 as a mass-market paperback.

The difference in reception of the two books cannot, we believe, be explained by a difference in quality. Indeed, the earlier book is the more philosophical and abstract, and hence more fundamental. *Free to Choose,* as we said in its Preface, has "more nuts and bolts, less theoretical framework." It complements, rather than replaces, *Capitalism and Freedom.* On a superficial level, the difference in reception can be attributed to the power of television. *Free to Choose* was based on and designed to accompany our PBS series of the same name, and there can be little doubt that the success of the TV series gave prominence to the book.

That explanation is superficial because the existence and success of the TV program itself is testimony to the change in the intellectual climate. We were never approached in the 1960s to do a TV series like Free to Choose. There would have been few if any sponsors for such a program. If, by any chance, such a program had been produced, there would have been no significant audience receptive to its views. No, the different reception of the later book and the success of the TV series are common consequences of the change in the climate of opinion. The ideas in our two books are still far from being in the intellectual mainstream, but they are now, at least, respectable in the intellectual community and very likely almost conventional among the broader public.

The change in the climate of opinion was not produced by this book or the many others, such as Hayek's *Road to Serfdom* and *Constitution of Liberty,* in the same philosophical tradition. For evidence of that, it is enough to point to the call for contributions to the symposium *Capitalism, Socialism and Democracy* issued by the editors of *Commentary* in

1978, which went in part: "The idea that there may be an inescapable connection between capitalism and democracy has recently begun to seem plausible to a number of intellectuals who once would have regarded such a view not only as wrong but even as politically dangerous." My contribution consisted of an extensive quotation from *Capitalism and Freedom*, a briefer one from Adam Smith, and a closing invitation: "Welcome aboard."[1] Even in 1978, of the 25 contributors to the symposium other than myself, only 9 expressed views that could be classified as sympathetic to the central message of *Capitalism and Freedom*.

The change in the climate of opinion was produced by experience, not by theory or philosophy. Russia and China, once the great hopes of the intellectual classes, had clearly gone sour. Great Britian, whose Fabian socialism exercised a dominant influence on American intellectuals, was in deep trouble. Closer to home, the intellectuals, always devotees of big government and by wide majorities supporters of the national Democratic party, had been disillusioned by the Vietnam War, particularly the role played by Presidents Kennedy and Johnson. Many of the great reform programs—such guidons of the past as welfare, public housing, support of trade unions, integration of schools, federal aid to education, affirmative action—were turning to ashes. As with the rest of the population, their pocketbooks were being hit with inflation and high taxes. These phenomena, not the persuasiveness of the ideas expressed in books dealing with principles, explain the transition from the overwhelming defeat of Barry Goldwater in 1964 to the overwhelming victory of Ronald Reagan in 1980—two men with essentially the same program and the same message.

What then is the role of books such as this? Twofold, in my opinion. First, to provide subject matter for bull sessions. As we wrote in the Preface to *Free to Choose*: "The only person who can truly persuade you is yourself. You must turn the issues over in your mind at leisure, consider the many arguments, let them simmer, and after a long time turn your preferences into convictions."

Second, and more basic, to keep options open until circumstances make change necessary. There is enormous inertia—a

[1] *Commentary*, April 1978, pp. 29–71.

tyranny of the status quo—in private and especially governmental arrangements. Only a crisis—actual or perceived—produces real change. When that crisis occurs, the actions that are taken depend on the ideas that are lying around. That, I believe, is our basic function: to develop alternatives to existing policies, to keep them alive and available until the politically impossible becomes politically inevitable.

A personal story will perhaps make my point. Sometime in the late 1960s I engaged in a debate at the University of Wisconsin with Leon Keyserling, an unreconstructed collectivist. His clinching blow, as he thought, was to make fun of my views as utterly reactionary, and he chose to do so by reading, from the end of chapter 2 of this book, the list of items that, I said, "cannot, so far as I can see, validly be justified in terms of the principles outlined above." He was doing very well with the audience of students as he went through my castigation of price supports, tariffs, and so on, until he came to point 11, "Conscription to man the military services in peacetime." That expression of my opposition to the draft brought ardent applause and lost him the audience and the debate.

Incidentally, the draft is the only item on my list of fourteen unjustified government activities that has so far been eliminated—and that victory is by no means final. In respect of many of the other items, we have moved still farther away from the principles espoused in this book—which is, on one hand, a reason why the climate of opinion has changed and, on the other, evidence that that change has so far had little practical effect. Evidence also that the fundamental thrust of this book is as pertinent to 1981 as to 1962, even though some examples and details may be outdated.

+

Preface

THIS BOOK IS A LONG-DELAYED PRODUCT of a series of lectures that I gave in June, 1956 at a conference at Wabash College directed by John Van Sickle and Benjamin Rogge and sponsored by the Volker Foundation. In subsequent years, I have given similar lectures at Volker conferences directed by Arthur Kemp, at Claremont College, directed by Clarence Philbrook, at the University of North Carolina, and directed by Richard Leftwich, at Oklahoma State University. In each case I covered the contents of the first two chapters of this book, dealing with principles, and then applied the principles to a varied set of special problems.

I am indebted to the directors of these conferences not only for inviting me to give the lectures, but even more for their criticisms and comments on them and for friendly pressure to write them up in tentative form, and to Richard Cornuelle, Kenneth Templeton, and Ivan Bierly of the Volker Foundation who were responsible for arranging the conferences. I am indebted also to the participants who, by their incisive probing and deep interest in the issues, and unquenchable intellectual enthusiasm, forced me to rethink many points and to correct many errors. This series of conferences stands out as among the most stimulating intellectual experiences of my life. Needless to say, there is probably not one of the directors of the conferences or participants in them who agrees with everything in this book. But I trust they will not be unwilling to assume some of the responsibility for it.

I owe the philosophy expressed in this book and much of its detail to many teachers, colleagues, and friends, above all to a distinguished group I have been privileged to be associated with at the University of Chicago: Frank H. Knight, Henry C. Simons, Lloyd W. Mints, Aaron Director, Friedrich A. Hayek, George J. Stigler. I ask their pardon for my failure to acknowledge specifically the many ideas of theirs which they will find expressed in this book. I have learned so much from them and what I have learned has become so much a part of my own thought that I would not know how to select points to footnote.

I dare not try to list the many others to whom I am indebted, lest I do some an injustice by inadvertently omitting their names. But I cannot refrain from mentioning my children, Janet and David, whose willingness to accept nothing on faith has forced me to express technical matters in simple language and thereby improved both my understanding of the points and, hopefully, my exposition. I hasten to add that they too accept only responsibility, not identity of views.

I have drawn freely from material already published. Chapter i is a revision of material published earlier under the title used for this book in Felix Morley (ed.), *Essays in Individuality* (University of Pennsylvania Press, 1958) and in still a different form under the same title in *The New Individualist Review*, Vol. I, No. 1 (April, 1961). Chapter vi is a revision of an article by the same title first published in Robert A. Solo (ed.), *Economics and the Public Interest* (Rutgers University Press, 1955). Bits and pieces of other chapters have been taken from various of my articles and books.

The refrain, "But for my wife, this book would not have been written," has become a commonplace in academic prefaces. In this case, it happens to be the literal truth. She pieced together the scraps of the various lectures, coalesced different versions, translated lectures into something more closely approaching written English, and has throughout been the driving force in getting the book finished. The acknowledgment on the title page is an understatement.

My secretary, Muriel A. Porter, has been an efficient and dependable resource in time of need, and I am very much in her debt. She typed most of the manuscript as well as many earlier drafts of part of it.

$+$

Introduction

I N A MUCH QUOTED PASSAGE in his inaugural address, President Kennedy said, "Ask not what your country can do for you — ask what you can do for your country." It is a striking sign of the temper of our times that the controversy about this passage centered on its origin and not on its content. Neither half of the statement expresses a relation between the citizen and his government that is worthy of the ideals of free men in a free society. The paternalistic "what your country can do for you" implies that government is the patron, the citizen the ward, a view that is at odds with the free man's belief in his own responsibility for his own destiny. The organismic, "what you can do for your country" implies that government is the master or the deity, the citizen, the servant or the votary. To the free man, the country is the collection of individuals who compose it, not something over and above them. He is proud of a common heritage and loyal to common traditions. But he regards government as a means, an instrumentality, neither a grantor of favors and gifts, nor a master or god to be blindly worshipped and served. He recognizes no national goal except as it is the consensus of the goals that the citizens severally serve. He recognizes no national purpose except as it is the consensus of the purposes for which the citizens severally strive.

The free man will ask neither what his country can do for him nor what he can do for his country. He will ask rather "What can I and my compatriots do through government" to help us discharge our individual responsibilities, to achieve our several goals and purposes, and above all, to protect our freedom? And he will accompany this question with another: How can we keep the government we create from becoming a Frankenstein that will destroy the very freedom we establish it to protect? Freedom is a rare and delicate plant. Our minds tell us, and history confirms, that the great threat to freedom is the concentration of power. Government is necessary to preserve our freedom, it is an instrument through which we can exercise our freedom; yet by concentrating power in political hands, it is also a threat to freedom. Even though the men who wield this power initially be of good will and even though they be not corrupted by the power they exercise, the power will both attract and form men of a different stamp.

How can we benefit from the promise of government while avoiding the threat to freedom? Two broad principles embodied in our Constitution give an answer that has preserved our freedom so far, though they have been violated repeatedly in practice while proclaimed as precept.

First, the scope of government must be limited. Its major function must be to protect our freedom both from the enemies outside our gates and from our fellow-citizens: to preserve law and order, to enforce private contracts, to foster competitive markets. Beyond this major function, government may enable us at times to accomplish jointly what we would find it more difficult or expensive to accomplish severally. However, any such use of government is fraught with danger. We should not and cannot avoid using government in this way. But there should be a clear and large balance of advantages before we do. By relying primarily on voluntary co-operation and private enterprise, in both economic and other activities, we can insure that the private sector is a check on the powers of the governmental sector and an effective protection of freedom of speech, of religion, and of thought.

The second broad principle is that government power must be dispersed. If government is to exercise power, better in the county than in the state, better in the state than in Washington. If I do not like what my local community does, be it in sewage disposal, or zoning, or schools, I can move to another local community, and though few may take this step, the mere possibility acts as a check. If I do not like what my state does, I can move to another. If I do not like what Washington imposes, I have few alternatives in this world of jealous nations.

The very difficulty of avoiding the enactments of the federal government is of course the great attraction of centralization to many of its proponents. It will enable them more effectively, they believe, to legislate programs that — as they see it — are in the interest of the public, whether it be the transfer of income from the rich to the poor or from private to governmental purposes. They are in a sense right. But this coin has two sides. The power to do good is also the power to do harm; those who control the power today may not tomorrow; and, more important, what one man regards as good, another may regard as harm. The great tragedy of the drive to centralization, as of the drive to extend the scope of government in general, is that it is mostly led by men of good will who will be the first to rue its consequences.

The preservation of freedom is the protective reason for limiting and decentralizing governmental power. But there is also a constructive reason. The great advances of civilization, whether in architecture or painting, in science or literature, in industry or agriculture, have never come from centralized government. Columbus did not set out to seek a new route to China in response to a majority directive of a parliament, though he was partly financed by an absolute monarch. Newton and Leibnitz; Einstein and Bohr; Shakespeare, Milton, and Pasternak; Whitney, McCormick, Edison, and Ford; Jane Addams, Florence Nightingale, and Albert Schweitzer; no one of these opened new frontiers in human knowledge and understanding, in literature, in technical possibilities, or in the relief of human misery in response to governmental directives. Their achievements were the product of individual genius, of strongly held minority views, of a social climate permitting variety and diversity.

Government can never duplicate the variety and diversity of individual action. At any moment in time, by imposing uniform standards in housing, or nutrition, or clothing, government could undoubtedly improve the level of living of many individuals; by imposing uniform standards in schooling, road construction, or sanitation, central government could undoubtedly improve the level of performance in many local areas and perhaps even on the average of all communities. But in the process, government would replace progress by stagnation, it would substitute uniform mediocrity for the variety essential for that experimentation which can bring tomorrow's laggards above today's mean.

This book discusses some of these great issues. Its major theme is the role of competitive capitalism — the organization of the bulk of economic activity through private enterprise operating in a free market — as a system of economic freedom and a necessary condition for political freedom. Its minor theme is the role that government should play in a society dedicated to freedom and relying primarily on the market to organize economic activity.

The first two chapters deal with these issues on an abstract level, in terms of principles rather than concrete application. The later chapters apply these principles to a variety of particular problems.

An abstract statement can conceivably be complete and exhaustive, though this ideal is certainly far from realized in the two chapters that follow. The application of the principles cannot even conceivably be exhaustive. Each day brings new problems and new circumstances. That is why the role of the state can never be spelled out once and for all in terms of specific functions. It is also why we need from time to time to re-examine the bearing of what we hope are unchanged principles on the problems of the day. A by-product is inevitably a retesting of the principles and a sharpening of our understanding of them.

It is extremely convenient to have a label for the political and economic viewpoint elaborated in this book. The rightful and proper label is liberalism. Unfortunately, "As a supreme, if unintended compliment, the enemies of the system of private enterprise have thought it wise to appropriate its label",[1] so that liberalism has, in the United States, come to have a very different meaning than it did in the nineteenth century or does today over much of the Continent of Europe.

As it developed in the late eighteenth and early nineteenth centuries, the intellectual movement that went under the name of liberalism emphasized freedom as the ultimate goal and the individual as the ultimate entity in the society. It supported laissez faire at home as a means of reducing the role of the state in economic affairs and thereby enlarging the role of the individual; it supported free trade abroad as a means of linking the nations of the world together peacefully and democratically. In political matters, it supported the development of representative government and of parliamentary institutions, reduction in the arbitrary power of the state, and protection of the civil freedoms of individuals.

Beginning in the late nineteenth century, and especially after 1930 in the United States, the term liberalism came to be associated with a very different emphasis, particularly in economic policy. It came to be associated with a readiness to rely primarily on the state rather than on private voluntary arrangements to achieve objectives regarded as desirable. The catchwords became welfare and equality rather than freedom. The nineteenth-century liberal regarded an extension of freedom as the most effective way to promote welfare and equality; the twentieth-century liberal regards welfare and equality as either prerequisites of or alternatives to freedom. In the name of welfare and equality, the twentieth-century liberal has come to favor a revival of the very policies of state intervention and paternalism

[1] Joseph Schumpeter, *History of Economic Analysis* (New York: Oxford University Press, 1954) p. 394.

against which classical liberalism fought. In the very act of turning the clock back to seventeenth-century mercantilism, he is fond of castigating true liberals as reactionary!

The change in the meaning attached to the term liberalism is more striking in economic matters than in political. The twentieth-century liberal, like the nineteenth-century liberal, favors parliamentary institutions, representative government, civil rights, and so on. Yet even in political matters, there is a notable difference. Jealous of liberty, and hence fearful of centralized power, whether in governmental or private hands, the nineteenth-century liberal favored political decentralization. Committed to action and confident of the beneficence of power so long as it is in the hands of a government ostensibly controlled by the electorate, the twentieth-century liberal favors centralized government. He will resolve any doubt about where power should be located in favor of the state instead of the city, of the federal government instead of the state, and of a world organization instead of a national government.

Because of the corruption of the term liberalism, the views that formerly went under that name are now often labeled conservatism. But this is not a satisfactory alternative. The nineteenth-century liberal was a radical, both in the etymological sense of going to the root of the matter, and in the political sense of favoring major changes in social institutions. So too must be his modern heir. We do not wish to conserve the state interventions that have interfered so greatly with our freedom, though, of course, we do wish to conserve those that have promoted it, Moreover, in practice, the term conservatism has come to cover so wide a range of views, and views so incompatible with one another, that we shall no doubt see the growth of hyphenated designations, such as libertarian-conservative and aristocratic-conservative.

Partly because of my reluctance to surrender the term to proponents of measures that would destroy liberty, partly because I cannot find a better alternative, I shall resolve these difficulties by using the word liberalism in its original sense — as the doctrines pertaining to a free man.

Chapter 1

The Relation between Economic Freedom and Political Freedom

It is widely believed that politics and economics are separate and largely unconnected; that individual freedom is a political problem and material welfare an economic problem; and that any kind of political arrangements can be combined with any kind of economic arrangements. The chief contemporary manifestation of this idea is the advocacy of "democratic socialism" by many who condemn out of hand the restrictions on individual freedom imposed by "totalitarian socialism" in Russia, and who are persuaded that it is possible for a country to adopt the essential features of Russian economic arrangements and yet to ensure individual freedom through political arrangements. The thesis of this chapter is that such a view is a delusion, that there is an intimate connection between economics and politics, that only certain combinations of political and economic arrangements are possible, and that in particular, a society which is socialist cannot also be democratic, in the sense of guaranteeing individual freedom.

Economic arrangements play a dual role in the promotion of a free society. On the one hand, freedom in economic arrangements is itself a component of freedom broadly understood, so economic freedom is an end in itself. In the second place, economic freedom is also an indispensable means toward the achievement of political freedom.

The first of these roles of economic freedom needs special emphasis because intellectuals in particular have a strong bias against regarding this aspect of freedom as important. They tend to express contempt for what they regard as material aspects of life, and to regard their own pursuit of allegedly higher values as on a different plane of significance and as deserving of special attention. For most citizens of the country, however, if not for the intellectual, the direct importance of economic freedom is at least comparable in significance to the indirect importance of economic freedom as a means to political freedom.

The citizen of Great Britain, who after World War II was not permitted to spend his vacation in the United States because of exchange control, was being deprived of an essential freedom no less than the citizen of the United States, who was denied the opportunity to spend his vacation in Russia because of his political views. The one was ostensibly an economic limitation on freedom and the other a political limitation, yet there is no essential difference between the two.

The citizen of the United States who is compelled by law to devote something like 10 per cent of his income to the purchase of a particular kind of retirement contract, administered by the government, is being deprived of a corresponding part of his personal freedom. How strongly this deprivation may be felt and its closeness to the deprivation of religious freedom, which all would regard as "civil" or "political" rather than "economic", were dramatized by an episode involving a group of farmers of the Amish sect. On grounds of principle, this group

regarded compulsory federal old age programs as an infringement of their personal individual freedom and refused to pay
taxes or accept benefits. As a result, some of their livestock were
sold by auction in order to satisfy claims for social security levies.
True, the number of citizens who regard compulsory old age
insurance as a deprivation of freedom may be few, but the believer in freedom has never counted noses.

A citizen of the United States who under the laws of various
states is not free to follow the occupation of his own choosing
unless he can get a license for it, is likewise being deprived of
an essential part of his freedom. So is the man who would like
to exchange some of his goods with, say, a Swiss for a watch but
is prevented from doing so by a quota. So also is the Californian
who was thrown into jail for selling Alka Seltzer at a price below
that set by the manufacturer under so-called "fair trade" laws.
So also is the farmer who cannot grow the amount of wheat he
wants. And so on. Clearly, economic freedom, in and of itself, is
an extremely important part of total freedom.

Viewed as a means to the end of political freedom, economic
arrangements are important because of their effect on the concentration or dispersion of power. The kind of economic organization that provides economic freedom directly, namely,
competitive capitalism, also promotes political freedom because
it separates economic power from political power and in this
way enables the one to offset the other.

Historical evidence speaks with a single voice on the relation
between political freedom and a free market. I know of no
example in time or place of a society that has been marked by a
large measure of political freedom, and that has not also used
something comparable to a free market to organize the bulk of
economic activity.

Because we live in a largely free society, we tend to forget how
limited is the span of time and the part of the globe for which
there has ever been anything like political freedom: the typical
state of mankind is tyranny, servitude, and misery. The nineteenth century and early twentieth century in the Western world
stand out as striking exceptions to the general trend of historical
development. Political freedom in this instance clearly came
along with the free market and the development of capitalist

institutions. So also did political freedom in the golden age of Greece and in the early days of the Roman era.

History suggests only that capitalism is a necessary condition for political freedom. Clearly it is not a sufficient condition. Fascist Italy and Fascist Spain, Germany at various times in the last seventy years, Japan before World Wars I and II, tzarist Russia in the decades before World War I — are all societies that cannot conceivably be described as politically free. Yet, in each, private enterprise was the dominant form of economic organization. It is therefore clearly possible to have economic arrangements that are fundamentally capitalist and political arrangements that are not free.

Even in those societies, the citizenry had a good deal more freedom than citizens of a modern totalitarian state like Russia or Nazi Germany, in which economic totalitarianism is combined with political totalitarianism. Even in Russia under the Tzars, it was possible for some citizens, under some circumstances, to change their jobs without getting permission from political authority because capitalism and the existence of private property provided some check to the centralized power of the state.

The relation between political and economic freedom is complex and by no means unilateral. In the early nineteenth century, Bentham and the Philosophical Radicals were inclined to regard political freedom as a means to economic freedom. They believed that the masses were being hampered by the restrictions that were being imposed upon them, and that if political reform gave the bulk of the people the vote, they would do what was good for them, which was to vote for laissez faire. In retrospect, one cannot say that they were wrong. There was a large measure of political reform that was accompanied by economic reform in the direction of a great deal of laissez faire. An enormous increase in the well-being of the masses followed this change in economic arrangements.

The triumph of Benthamite liberalism in nineteenth-century England was followed by a reaction toward increasing intervention by government in economic affairs. This tendency to collectivism was greatly accelerated, both in England and elsewhere, by the two World Wars. Welfare rather than freedom became the dominant note in democratic countries. Recognizing the implicit threat to individualism, the intellectual descendants of the Philosophical Radicals — Dicey, Mises, Hayek, and Simons, to mention only a few — feared that a continued movement toward centralized control of economic activity would prove *The Road to Serfdom*, as Hayek entitled his penetrating analysis of the process. Their emphasis was on economic freedom as a means toward political freedom.

Events since the end of World War II display still a different relation between economic and political freedom. Collectivist economic planning has indeed interfered with individual freedom. At least in some countries, however, the result has not been the suppression of freedom, but the reversal of economic policy. England again provides the most striking example. The turning point was perhaps the "control of engagements" order which, despite great misgivings, the Labour party found it necessary to impose in order to carry out its economic policy. Fully enforced and carried through, the law would have involved centralized allocation of individuals to occupations. This conflicted so sharply with personal liberty that it was enforced in a negligible number of cases, and then repealed after the law had been in effect for only a short period. Its repeal ushered in a decided shift in economic policy, marked by reduced reliance on centralized "plans" and "programs", by the dismantling of many controls, and by increased emphasis on the private market. A similar shift in policy occurred in most other democratic countries.

The proximate explanation of these shifts in policy is the limited success of central planning or its outright failure to achieve stated objectives. However, this failure is itself to be attributed, at least in some measure, to the political implications of central planning and to an unwillingness to follow out its logic when doing so requires trampling rough-shod on treasured private rights. It may well be that the shift is only a temporary interruption in the collectivist trend of this century. Even so, it illustrates the close relation between political freedom and economic arrangements.

Historical evidence by itself can never be convincing. Perhaps it was sheer coincidence that the expansion of freedom occurred at the same time as the development of capitalist and market institutions. Why should there be a connection? What are the logical links between economic and political freedom? In discussing these questions we shall consider first the market as a direct component of freedom, and then the indirect relation between market arrangements and political freedom. A by-product will be an outline of the ideal economic arrangements for a free society.

As liberals, we take freedom of the individual, or perhaps the family, as our ultimate goal in judging social arrangements. Freedom as a value in this sense has to do with the interrelations among people; it has no meaning whatsoever to a Robinson Crusoe on an isolated island (without his Man Friday). Robinson Crusoe on his island is subject to "constraint," he has limited "power," and he has only a limited number of alternatives, but there is no problem of freedom in the sense that is relevant to our discussion. Similarly, in a society freedom has nothing to say about what an individual does with his freedom; it is not an all-embracing ethic. Indeed, a major aim of the liberal is to leave the ethical problem for the individual to wrestle with. The "really" important ethical problems are those that face an individual in a free society — what he should do with his freedom. There are thus two sets of values that a liberal will emphasize — the values that are relevant to relations among people, which is the context in which he assigns first priority to freedom; and the values that are relevant to the individual in the exercise of his freedom, which is the realm of individual ethics and philosophy.

The liberal conceives of men as imperfect beings. He regards the problem of social organization to be as much a negative problem of preventing "bad" people from doing harm as of enabling "good" people to do good; and, of course, "bad" and "good" people may be the same people, depending on who is judging them.

The basic problem of social organization is how to co-ordinate the economic activities of large numbers of people. Even in relatively backward societies, extensive division of labor and specialization of function is required to make effective use of available resources. In advanced societies, the scale on which co-ordination is needed, to take full advantage of the opportunities offered by modern science and technology, is enormously greater. Literally millions of people are involved in providing one another with their daily bread, let alone with their yearly automobiles. The challenge to the believer in liberty is to reconcile this widespread interdependence with individual freedom.

Fundamentally, there are only two ways of co-ordinating the economic activities of millions. One is central direction involving the use of coercion — the technique of the army and of the modern totalitarian state. The other is voluntary co-operation of individuals — the technique of the market place.

The possibility of co-ordination through voluntary co-operation rests on the elementary — yet frequently denied — proposition that both parties to an economic transaction benefit from it, *provided the transaction is bi-laterally voluntary and informed.*

Exchange can therefore bring about co-ordination without coercion. A working model of a society organized through voluntary exchange is a *free private enterprise exchange economy* — what we have been calling competitive capitalism.

In its simplest form, such a society consists of a number of independent households — a collection of Robinson Crusoes, as it were. Each household uses the resources it controls to produce goods and services that it exchanges for goods and services produced by other households, on terms mutually acceptable to the two parties to the bargain. It is thereby enabled to satisfy its wants indirectly by producing goods and services for others, rather than directly by producing goods for its own immediate use. The incentive for adopting this indirect route is, of course, the increased product made possible by division of labor and specialization of function. Since the household always has the alternative of producing directly for itself, it need not enter into any exchange unless it benefits from it. Hence, no exchange will take place unless both parties do benefit from it. Co-operation is thereby achieved without coercion.

Specialization of function and division of labor would not go far if the ultimate productive unit were the household. In a modern society, we have gone much farther. We have introduced enterprises which are intermediaries between individuals in their capacities as suppliers of service and as purchasers of goods. And similarly, specialization of function and division of labor could not go very far if we had to continue to rely on the barter of product for product. In consequence, money has been introduced as a means of facilitating exchange, and of enabling the acts of purchase and of sale to be separated into two parts.

Despite the important role of enterprises and of money in our actual economy, and despite the numerous and complex problems they raise, the central characteristic of the market technique of achieving co-ordination is fully displayed in the simple exchange economy that contains neither enterprises nor money. As in that simple model, so in the complex enterprise and money-exchange economy, co-operation is strictly individual and voluntary *provided*: (*a*) that enterprises are private, so that the ultimate contracting parties are individuals and (*b*) that individuals are effectively free to enter or not to enter into any particular exchange, so that every transaction is strictly voluntary.

It is far easier to state these provisos in general terms than to spell them out in detail, or to specify precisely the institutional arrangements most conducive to their maintenance. Indeed, much of technical economic literature is concerned with precisely these questions. The basic requisite is the maintenance of law and order to prevent physical coercion of one individual by another and to enforce contracts voluntarily entered into, thus giving substance to "private". Aside from this, perhaps the most difficult problems arise from monopoly — which inhibits effective freedom by denying individuals alternatives to the particular exchange — and from "neighborhood effects" — effects on third parties for which it is not feasible to charge or recompense them. These problems will be discussed in more detail in the following chapter.

So long as effective freedom of exchange is maintained, the central feature of the market organization of economic activity is that it prevents one person from interfering with another in respect of most of his activities. The consumer is protected from coercion by the seller because of the presence of other sellers with whom he can deal. The seller is protected from coercion by the consumer because of other consumers to whom he can sell. The employee is protected from coercion by the employer because of other employers for whom he can work, and so on. And the market does this impersonally and without centralized authority.

Indeed, a major source of objection to a free economy is precisely that it does this task so well. It gives people what they want instead of what a particular group thinks they ought to want. Underlying most arguments against the free market is a lack of belief in freedom itself.

The existence of a free market does not of course eliminate the need for government. On the contrary, government is essential both as a forum for determining the "rules of the game" and as an umpire to interpret and enforce the rules decided on. What the market does is to reduce greatly the range of issues that must be decided through political means, and thereby to minimize the extent to which government need participate directly in the game. The characteristic feature of action through political channels is that it tends to require or enforce substantial conformity. The great advantage of the market, on the other hand, is that it permits wide diversity. It is, in political terms, a system of proportional representation. Each man can vote, as it were, for the color of tie he wants and get it; he does not have to see what color the majority wants and then, if he is in the minority, submit.

It is this feature of the market that we refer to when we say that the market provides economic freedom. But this characteristic also has implications that go far beyond the narrowly economic. Political freedom means the absence of coercion of a man by his fellow men. The fundamental threat to freedom is power to coerce, be it in the hands of a monarch, a dictator, an oligarchy, or a momentary majority. The preservation of freedom requires the elimination of such concentration of power to the fullest possible extent and the dispersal and distribution of whatever power cannot be eliminated — a system of checks and balances. By removing the organization of economic activity from the control of political authority, the market eliminates this source of coercive power. It enables economic strength to be a check to political power rather than a reinforcement.

Economic power can be widely dispersed. There is no law of conservation which forces the growth of new centers of economic strength to be at the expense of existing centers. Political power, on the other hand, is more difficult to decentralize. There can be numerous small independent governments. But it is far more difficult to maintain numerous equipotent small centers of political power in a single large government than it is to have numerous centers of economic strength in a single large economy. There can be many millionaires in one large economy. But can there be more than one really outstanding leader, one person on whom the energies and enthusiasms of his countrymen are centered? If the central government gains power, it is likely to be at the expense of local governments. There seems to be something like a fixed total of political power to be distributed. Consequently, if economic power is joined to political power, concentration seems almost inevitable. On the other hand, if economic power is kept in separate hands from political power, it can serve as a check and a counter to political power.

The force of this abstract argument can perhaps best be demonstrated by example. Let us consider first, a hypothetical example that may help to bring out the principles involved, and then some actual examples from recent experience that illustrate the way in which the market works to preserve political freedom.

One feature of a free society is surely the freedom of individuals to advocate and propagandize openly for a radical change in the structure of the society — so long as the advocacy is restricted to persuasion and does not include force or other forms of coercion. It is a mark of the political freedom of a capitalist society that men can openly advocate and work for socialism. Equally, political freedom in a socialist society would require that men be free to advocate the introduction of capitalism. How could the freedom to advocate capitalism be preserved and protected in a socialist society?

In order for men to advocate anything, they must in the first place be able to earn a living. This already raises a problem in a socialist society, since all jobs are under the direct control of political authorities. It would take an act of self-denial whose difficulty is underlined by experience in the United States after World War II with the problem of "security" among Federal employees, for a socialist government to permit its employees to advocate policies directly contrary to official doctrine.

But let us suppose this act of self-denial to be achieved. For advocacy of capitalism to mean anything, the proponents must be able to finance their cause — to hold public meetings, publish pamphlets, buy radio time, issue newspapers and magazines, and so on. How could they raise the funds? There might and probably would be men in the socialist society with large incomes, perhaps even large capital sums in the form of government bonds and the like, but these would of necessity be high public officials. It is possible to conceive of a minor socialist official retaining his job although openly advocating capitalism. It strains credulity to imagine the socialist top brass financing such "subversive" activities.

The only recourse for funds would be to raise small amounts from a large number of minor officials. But this is no real answer. To tap these sources, many people would already have to be persuaded, and our whole problem is how to initiate and finance a campaign to do so. Radical movements in capitalist societies have never been financed this way. They have typically been supported by a few wealthy individuals who have become persuaded — by a Frederick Vanderbilt Field, or an Anita McCormick Blaine, or a Corliss Lamont, to mention a few names recently prominent, or by a Friedrich Engels, to go farther back. This is a role of inequality of wealth in preserving political freedom that is seldom noted — the role of the patron.

In a capitalist society, it is only necessary to convince a few wealthy people to get funds to launch any idea, however strange, and there are many such persons, many independent foci of support. And, indeed, it is not even necessary to persuade people or financial institutions with available funds of the soundness of the ideas to be propagated. It is only necessary to persuade them that the propagation can be financially successful; that the newspaper or magazine or book or other venture will be profitable. The competitive publisher, for example, cannot afford to publish only writing with which he personally agrees; his touchstone must be the likelihood that the market will be large enough to yield a satisfactory return on his investment.

In this way, the market breaks the vicious circle and makes it possible ultimately to finance such ventures by small amounts from many people without first persuading them. There are no such possibilities in the socialist society; there is only the all-powerful state.

Let us stretch our imagination and suppose that a socialist government is aware of this problem and is composed of people anxious to preserve freedom. Could it provide the funds? Perhaps, but it is difficult to see how. It could establish a bureau for subsidizing subversive propaganda. But how could it choose whom to support? If it gave to all who asked, it would shortly find itself out of funds, for socialism cannot repeal the elementary economic law that a sufficiently high price will call forth a large supply. Make the advocacy of radical causes sufficiently remunerative, and the supply of advocates will be unlimited.

Moreover, freedom to advocate unpopular causes does not require that such advocacy be without cost. On the contrary, no society could be stable if advocacy of radical change were costless, much less subsidized. It is entirely appropriate that men make sacrifices to advocate causes in which they deeply believe. Indeed, it is important to preserve freedom only for people who are willing to practice self-denial, for otherwise freedom degenerates into license and irresponsibility. What is essential is that the cost of advocating unpopular causes be tolerable and not prohibitive.

But we are not yet through. In a free market society, it is enough to have the funds. The suppliers of paper are as willing to sell it to the *Daily Worker* as to the *Wall Street Journal*. In a socialist society, it would not be enough to have the funds. The hypothetical supporter of capitalism would have to persuade a government factory making paper to sell to him, the government printing press to print his pamphlets, a government post office to distribute them among the people, a government agency to rent him a hall in which to talk, and so on.

Perhaps there is some way in which one could overcome these difficulties and preserve freedom in a socialist society. One cannot say it is utterly impossible. What is clear, however, is that there are very real difficulties in establishing institutions that will effectively preserve the possibility of dissent. So far as I know, none of the people who have been in favor of socialism and also in favor of freedom have really faced up to this issue, or made even a respectable start at developing the institutional arrangements that would permit freedom under socialism. By contrast, it is clear how a free market capitalist society fosters freedom.

A striking practical example of these abstract principles is the experience of Winston Churchill. From 1933 to the outbreak of World War II, Churchill was not permitted to talk over the British radio, which was, of course, a government monopoly administered by the British Broadcasting Corporation. Here was a leading citizen of his country, a Member of Parliament, a former cabinet minister, a man who was desperately trying by every device possible to persuade his countrymen to take steps to ward off the menace of Hitler's Germany. He was not permitted to talk over the radio to the British people because the BBC was a government monopoly and his position was too "controversial".

Another striking example, reported in the January 26, 1959 issue of *Time*, has to do with the "Blacklist Fadeout". Says the *Time* story,

The Oscar-awarding ritual is Hollywood's biggest pitch for dignity, but two years ago dignity suffered. When one Robert Rich was announced as top writer for the *The Brave One*, he never stepped forward. Robert Rich was a pseudonym, masking one of about 150 writers . . . blacklisted by the industry since 1947 as suspected Communists or fellow travelers. The case was particularly embarrassing because the Motion Picture Academy had barred any Communist or Fifth Amendment pleader from Oscar competition. Last week both the Communist rule and the mystery of Rich's identity were suddenly rescripted.

Rich turned out to be Dalton (*Johnny Got His Gun*) Trumbo, one of the original "Hollywood Ten" writers who refused to testify at the 1947 hearings on Communism in the movie industry. Said producer Frank King, who had stoutly insisted that Robert Rich was "a young guy in Spain with a beard": "We have an obligation to our stockholders to buy the best script we can. Trumbo brought us *The Brave One* and we bought it". . . .

In effect it was the formal end of the Hollywood black list. For barred writers, the informal end came long ago. At least 15% of current Hollywood films are reportedly written by blacklist members. Said Producer King, "There are more ghosts in Hollywood than in Forest Lawn. Every company in town has used the work of blacklisted people. We're just the first to confirm what everybody knows."

One may believe, as I do, that communism would destroy all of our freedoms, one may be opposed to it as firmly and as strongly as possible, and yet, at the same time, also believe that in a free society it is intolerable for a man to be prevented from making voluntary arrangements with others that are mutually attractive because he believes in or is trying to promote communism. His freedom includes his freedom to promote communism. Freedom also, of course, includes the freedom of others not to deal with him under those circumstances. The Hollywood blacklist was an unfree act that destroys freedom because it was a collusive arrangement that used coercive means to prevent voluntary exchanges. It didn't work precisely because the market made it costly for people to preserve the blacklist. The commercial emphasis, the fact that people who are running enterprises have an incentive to make as much money as they can, protected the freedom of the individuals who were blacklisted by providing them with an alternative form of employment, and by giving people an incentive to employ them.

If Hollywood and the movie industry had been government enterprises or if in England it had been a question of employment by the British Broadcasting Corporation it is difficult to believe that the "Hollywood Ten" or their equivalent would have found employment. Equally, it is difficult to believe that under those circumstances, strong proponents of individualism and private enterprise — or indeed strong proponents of any view other than the status quo — would be able to get employment.

Another example of the role of the market in preserving political freedom, was revealed in our experience with McCarthyism. Entirely aside from the substantive issues involved, and the merits of the charges made, what protection did individuals, and in particular government employees, have against irresponsible accusations and probings into matters that it went against their conscience to reveal? Their appeal to the Fifth Amendment would have been a hollow mockery without an alternative to government employment.

Their fundamental protection was the existence of a private-market economy in which they could earn a living. Here again, the protection was not absolute. Many potential private employers were, rightly or wrongly, averse to hiring those pilloried. It may well be that there was far less justification for the costs imposed on many of the people involved than for the costs generally imposed on people who advocate unpopular causes. But the important point is that the costs were limited and not prohibitive, as they would have been if government employment had been the only possibility.

It is of interest to note that a disproportionately large fraction of the people involved apparently went into the most competitive sectors of the economy — small business, trade, farming — where the market approaches most closely the ideal free market. No one who buys bread knows whether the wheat from which it is made was grown by a Communist or a Republican, by a constitutionalist or a Fascist, or, for that matter, by a Negro or a white. This illustrates how an impersonal market separates economic activities from political views and protects men from being discriminated against in their economic activities for reasons that are irrelevant to their productivity — whether these reasons are associated with their views or their color.

As this example suggests, the groups in our society that have the most at stake in the preservation and strengthening of competitive capitalism are those minority groups which can most easily become the object of the distrust and enmity of the majority — the Negroes, the Jews, the foreign-born, to mention only the most obvious. Yet, paradoxically enough, the enemies of the free market — the Socialists and Communists — have been recruited in disproportionate measure from these groups. Instead of recognizing that the existence of the market has protected them from the attitudes of their fellow countrymen, they mistakenly attribute the residual discrimination to the market.

Chapter II

The Role of Government
in a Free Society

A COMMON OBJECTION to totalitarian societies is that they regard the end as justifying the means. Taken literally, this objection is clearly illogical. If the end does not justify the means, what does? But this easy answer does not dispose of the objection; it simply shows that the objection is not well put. To deny that the end justifies the means is indirectly to assert that the end in question is not the ultimate end, that the ultimate end is itself the use of the proper means. Desirable or not, any end that can be attained only by the use of bad means must give way to the more basic end of the use of acceptable means.

To the liberal, the appropriate means are free discussion and voluntary co-operation, which implies that any form of coercion is inappropriate. The ideal is unanimity among responsible individuals achieved on the basis of free and full discussion. This is another way of expressing the goal of freedom emphasized in the preceding chapter.

From this standpoint, the role of the market, as already noted, is that it permits unanimity without conformity; that it is a system of effectively proportional representation. On the other hand, the characteristic feature of action through explicitly political channels is that it tends to require or to enforce substantial conformity. The typical issue must be decided "yes" or "no"; at most, provision can be made for a fairly limited number of alternatives. Even the use of proportional representation in its explicitly political form does not alter this conclusion. The number of separate groups that can in fact be represented is narrowly limited, enormously so by comparison with the proportional representation of the market. More important, the fact that the final outcome generally must be a law applicable to all groups, rather than separate legislative enactments for each "party" represented, means that proportional representation in its political version, far from permitting unanimity without conformity, tends toward ineffectiveness and fragmentation. It thereby operates to destroy any consensus on which unanimity with conformity can rest.

There are clearly some matters with respect to which effective proportional representation is impossible. I cannot get the amount of national defense I want and you, a different amount. With respect to such indivisible matters we can discuss, and argue, and vote. But having decided, we must conform. It is precisely the existence of such indivisible matters — protection of the individual and the nation from coercion are clearly the most basic — that prevents exclusive reliance on individual action through the market. If we are to use some of our resources for such indivisible items, we must employ political channels to reconcile differences.

The use of political channels, while inevitable, tends to strain the social cohesion essential for a stable society. The strain is least if agreement for joint action need be reached only on a limited range of issues on which people in any event have common views. Every extension of the range of issues for which explicit agreement is sought strains further the delicate threads that hold society together. If it goes so far as to touch an issue on which men feel deeply yet differently, it may well disrupt the society. Fundamental differences in basic values can seldom if ever be resolved at the ballot box; ultimately they can only be decided, though not resolved, by conflict. The religious and civil wars of history are a bloody testament to this judgment.

The widespread use of the market reduces the strain on the social fabric by rendering conformity unnecessary with respect to any activities it encompasses. The wider the range of activities covered by the market, the fewer are the issues on which explicitly political decisions are required and hence on which it is necessary to achieve agreement. In turn, the fewer the issues on which agreement is necessary, the greater is the likelihood of getting agreement while maintaining a free society.

Unanimity is, of course, an ideal. In practice, we can afford neither the time nor the effort that would be required to achieve complete unanimity on every issue. We must perforce accept something less. We are thus led to accept majority rule in one form or another as an expedient. That majority rule is an expedient rather than itself a basic principle is clearly shown by the fact that our willingness to resort to majority rule, and the size of the majority we require, themselves depend on the seriousness of the issue involved. If the matter is of little moment and the minority has no strong feelings about being overruled, a bare plurality will suffice. On the other hand, if the minority feels strongly about the issue involved, even a bare majority will not do. Few of us would be willing to have issues of free speech, for example, decided by a bare majority. Our legal structure is full of such distinctions among kinds of issues that require different kinds of majorities. At the extreme are those issues embodied in the Constitution. These are the principles that are so important that we are willing to make minimal concessions to expediency. Something like essential consensus was achieved initially in accepting them, and we require something like essential consensus for a change in them.

The self-denying ordinance to refrain from majority rule on certain kinds of issues that is embodied in our Constitution and in similar written or unwritten constitutions elsewhere, and the specific provisions in these constitutions or their equivalents prohibiting coercion of individuals, are themselves to be regarded as reached by free discussion and as reflecting essential unanimity about means.

I turn now to consider more specifically, though still in very broad terms, what the areas are that cannot be handled through the market at all, or can be handled only at so great a cost that the use of political channels may be preferable.

GOVERNMENT AS RULE-MAKER AND UMPIRE

It is important to distinguish the day-to-day activities of people from the general customary and legal framework within which these take place. The day-to-day activities are like the actions of the participants in a game when they are playing it; the framework, like the rules of the game they play. And just as a good game requires acceptance by the players both of the rules and of the umpire to interpret and enforce them, so a good society requires that its members agree on the general conditions that will govern relations among them, on some means of arbitrating different interpretations of these conditions, and on some device for enforcing compliance with the generally accepted rules. As in games, so also in society, most of the general conditions are the unintended outcome of custom, accepted unthinkingly. At most, we consider explicitly only minor modifications in them, though the cumulative effect of a series of minor modifications may be a drastic alteration in the character of the game or of the society. In both games and society also, no set of rules can prevail unless most participants most of the time conform to them without external sanctions; unless that is, there is a broad underlying social consensus. But we cannot rely on custom or on this consensus alone to interpret and to enforce the rules; we need an umpire. These then are the basic roles of government in a free society: to provide a means whereby we can modify the rules, to mediate differences among us on the meaning of the rules, and to enforce compliance with the rules on the part of those few who would otherwise not play the game.

The need for government in these respects arises because absolute freedom is impossible. However attractive anarchy may be as a philosophy, it is not feasible in a world of imperfect men.

Men's freedoms can conflict, and when they do, one man's freedom must be limited to preserve another's — as a Supreme Court Justice once put it, "My freedom to move my fist must be limited by the proximity of your chin."

The major problem in deciding the appropriate activities of government is how to resolve such conflicts among the freedoms of different individuals. In some cases, the answer is easy. There is little difficulty in attaining near unanimity to the proposition that one man's freedom to murder his neighbor must be sacrificed to preserve the freedom of the other man to live. In other cases, the answer is difficult. In the economic area, a major problem arises in respect of the conflict between freedom to combine and freedom to compete. What meaning is to be attributed to "free" as modifying "enterprise"? In the United States, "free" has been understood to mean that anyone is free to set up an enterprise, which means that existing enterprises are not free to keep out competitors except by selling a better product at the same price or the same product at a lower price. In the continental tradition, on the other hand, the meaning has generally been that enterprises are free to do what they want, including the fixing of prices, division of markets, and the adoption of other techniques to keep out potential competitors. Perhaps the most difficult specific problem in this area arises with respect to combinations among laborers, where the problem of freedom to combine and freedom to compete is particularly acute.

A still more basic economic area in which the answer is both difficult and important is the definition of property rights. The notion of property, as it has developed over centuries and as it is embodied in our legal codes, has become so much a part of us that we tend to take it for granted, and fail to recognize the extent to which just what constitutes property and what rights the ownership of property confers are complex social creations rather than self-evident propositions. Does my having title to land, for example, and my freedom to use my property as I wish, permit me to deny to someone else the right to fly over my land in his airplane? Or does his right to use his airplane take precedence? Or does this depend on how high he flies? Or how much noise he makes? Does voluntary exchange require that he pay me for the privilege of flying over my land? Or that I must pay him to refrain from flying over it? The mere mention of royalties, copyrights, patents; shares of stock in corporations; riparian rights, and the like, may perhaps emphasize the role of generally accepted social rules in the very definition of property. It may suggest also that, in many cases, the existence of a well specified and generally accepted definition of property is far more important than just what the definition is.

Another economic area that raises particularly difficult problems is the monetary system. Government responsibility for the monetary system has long been recognized. It is explicitly provided for in the constitutional provision which gives Congress the power "to coin money, regulate the value thereof, and of foreign coin." There is probably no other area of economic activity with respect to which government action has been so uniformly accepted. This habitual and by now almost unthinking acceptance of governmental responsibility makes thorough understanding of the grounds for such responsibility all the more necessary, since it enhances the danger that the scope of government will spread from activities that are, to those that are not, appropriate in a free society, from providing a monetary framework to determining the allocation of resources among individuals. We shall discuss this problem in detail in chapter iii.

In summary, the organization of economic activity through voluntary exchange presumes that we have provided, through government, for the maintenance of law and order to prevent coercion of one individual by another, the enforcement of contracts voluntarily entered into, the definition of the meaning of property rights, the interpretation and enforcement of such rights, and the provision of a monetary framework.

ACTION THROUGH GOVERNMENT ON GROUNDS OF
TECHNICAL MONOPOLY AND NEIGHBORHOOD EFFECTS

The role of government just considered is to do something that the market cannot do for itself, namely, to determine, arbitrate, and enforce the rules of the game. We may also want to do through government some things that might conceivably be done through the market but that technical or similar conditions render it difficult to do in that way. These all reduce to cases in which strictly voluntary exchange is either exceedingly costly or practically impossible. There are two general classes of such cases: monopoly and similar market imperfections, and neighborhood effects.

Exchange is truly voluntary only when nearly equivalent alternatives exist. Monopoly implies the absence of alternatives and thereby inhibits effective freedom of exchange. In practice, monopoly frequently, if not generally, arises from government support or from collusive agreements among individuals. With respect to these, the problem is either to avoid governmental fostering of monopoly or to stimulate the effective enforcement of rules such as those embodied in our anti-trust laws. However, monopoly may also arise because it is technically efficient to have a single producer or enterprise. I venture to suggest that such cases are more limited than is supposed but they unquestionably do arise. A simple example is perhaps the provision of telephone services within a community. I shall refer to such cases as "technical" monopoly.

When technical conditions make a monopoly the natural outcome of competitive market forces, there are only three alternatives that seem available: private monopoly, public monopoly, or public regulation. All three are bad so we must choose among evils. Henry Simons, observing public regulation of monopoly in the United States, found the results so distasteful that he concluded public monopoly would be a lesser evil. Walter Eucken, a noted German liberal, observing public monopoly in German railroads, found the results so distasteful that he concluded public regulation would be a lesser evil. Having learned from both, I reluctantly conclude that, if tolerable, private monopoly may be the least of the evils.

If society were static so that the conditions which give rise to a technical monopoly were sure to remain, I would have little confidence in this solution. In a rapidly changing society, however, the conditions making for technical monopoly frequently change and I suspect that both public regulation and public monopoly are likely to be less responsive to such changes in conditions, to be less readily capable of elimination, than private monopoly.

Railroads in the United States are an excellent example. A large degree of monopoly in railroads was perhaps inevitable on technical grounds in the nineteenth century. This was the justification for the Interstate Commerce Commission. But conditions have changed. The emergence of road and air transport has reduced the monopoly element in railroads to negligible proportions. Yet we have not eliminated the ICC. On the contrary, the ICC, which started out as an agency to protect the public from exploitation by the railroads, has become an agency to protect railroads from competition by trucks and other means of transport, and more recently even to protect existing truck companies from competition by new entrants. Similarly, in England, when the railroads were nationalized, trucking was at first brought into the state monopoly. If railroads had never been subjected to regulation in the United States, it is nearly certain that by now transportation, including railroads, would be a highly competitive industry with little or no remaining monopoly elements.

The choice between the evils of private monopoly, public monopoly, and public regulation cannot, however, be made once and for all, independently of the factual circumstances. If the technical monopoly is of a service or commodity that is regarded as essential and if its monopoly power is sizable, even the short-run effects of private unregulated monopoly may not be tolerable, and either public regulation or ownership may be a lesser evil.

Technical monopoly may on occasion justify a *de facto* public monopoly. It cannot by itself justify a public monopoly achieved by making it illegal for anyone else to compete. For example, there is no way to justify our present public monopoly of the post office. It may be argued that the carrying of mail is a technical monopoly and that a government monopoly is the least of evils. Along these lines, one could perhaps justify a government post office but not the present law, which makes it illegal for anybody else to carry mail. If the delivery of mail is a technical monopoly, no one will be able to suceed in competition with the government. If it is not, there is no reason why the government should be engaged in it. The only way to find out is to leave other people free to enter.

The historical reason why we have a post office monopoly is because the Pony Express did such a good job of carrying the mail across the continent that, when the government introduced transcontinental service, it couldn't compete effectively and lost money. The result was a law making it illegal for anybody else to carry the mail. That is why the Adams Express Company is an investment trust today instead of an operating company. I conjecture that if entry into the mail-carrying business were open to all, there would be a large number of firms entering it and this archaic industry would become revolutionized in short order.

A second general class of cases in which strictly voluntary exchange is impossible arises when actions of individuals have effects on other individuals for which it is not feasible to charge or recompense them. This is the problem of "neighborhood effects". An obvious example is the pollution of a stream. The man who pollutes a stream is in effect forcing others to exchange good water for bad. These others might be willing to make the exchange at a price. But it is not feasible for them, acting individually, to avoid the exchange or to enforce appropriate compensation.

A less obvious example is the provision of highways. In this case, it is technically possible to identify and hence charge individuals for their use of the roads and so to have private operation. However, for general access roads, involving many points of entry and exit, the costs of collection would be extremely high if a charge were to be made for the specific services received by each individual, because of the necessity of establishing toll booths or the equivalent at all entrances. The gasoline tax is a much cheaper method of charging individuals roughly in proportion to their use of the roads. This method, however, is one in which the particular payment cannot be identified closely with the particular use. Hence, it is hardly feasible to have private enterprise provide the service and collect the charge without establishing extensive private monopoly.

These considerations do not apply to long-distance turnpikes with high density of traffic and limited access. For these, the costs of collection are small and in many cases are now being paid, and there are often numerous alternatives, so that there is no serious monopoly problem. Hence, there is every reason why these should be privately owned and operated. If so owned and operated, the enterprise running the highway should receive the gasoline taxes paid on account of travel on it.

Parks are an interesting example because they illustrate the difference between cases that can and cases that cannot be justified by neighborhood effects, and because almost everyone at first sight regards the conduct of National Parks as obviously a valid function of government. In fact, however, neighborhood effects may justify a city park; they do not justify a national park, like Yellowstone National Park or the Grand Canyon. What is the fundamental difference between the two? For the city park, it is extremely difficult to identify the people who benefit from it and to charge them for the benefits which they receive. If there is a park in the middle of the city, the houses on all sides get the benefit of the open space, and people who walk through it or by it also benefit. To maintain toll collectors at the gates or to impose annual charges per window overlooking the park would be very expensive and difficult. The entrances to a national park like Yellowstone, on the other hand, are few; most of the people who come stay for a considerable period of time and it is perfectly feasible to set up toll gates and collect admission charges. This is indeed now done, though the charges do not cover the whole costs. If the public wants this kind of an activity enough to pay for it, private enterprises will have every incentive to provide such parks. And, of course, there are many private enterprises of this nature now in existence. I cannot myself conjure up any neighborhood effects or important monopoly effects that would justify governmental activity in this area.

Considerations like those I have treated under the heading of neighborhood effects have been used to rationalize almost every conceivable intervention. In many instances, however, this rationalization is special pleading rather than a legitimate application of the concept of neighborhood effects. Neighborhood effects cut both ways. They can be a reason for limiting the activities of government as well as for expanding them. Neighborhood effects impede voluntary exchange because it is difficult to identify the effects on third parties and to measure their magnitude; but this difficulty is present in governmental activity as well. It is hard to know when neighborhood effects are sufficiently large to justify particular costs in overcoming them and even harder to distribute the costs in an appropriate fashion. Consequently, when government engages in activities to overcome neighborhood effects, it will in part introduce an additional set of neighborhood effects by failing to charge or to compensate individuals properly. Whether the original or the new neighborhood effects are the more serious can only be judged by the facts of the individual case, and even then, only very approximately. Furthermore, the use of government to overcome neighborhood effects itself has an extremely important neighborhood effect which is unrelated to the particular occasion for government action. Every act of government intervention limits the area of individual freedom directly and threatens the preservation of freedom indirectly for reasons elaborated in the first chapter.

Our principles offer no hard and fast line how far it is appropriate to use government to accomplish jointly what it is difficult or impossible for us to accomplish separately through strictly voluntary exchange. In any particular case of proposed intervention, we must make up a balance sheet, listing separately the advantages and disadvantages. Our principles tell us what items to put on the one side and what items on the other and they give us some basis for attaching importance to the different items. In particular, we shall always want to enter on the liability side of any proposed government intervention, its neighborhood effect in threatening freedom, and give this effect considerable weight. Just how much weight to give to it, as to other items, depends upon the circumstances. If, for example, existing government intervention is minor, we shall attach a smaller weight to the negative effects of additional government intervention. This is an important reason why many earlier liberals, like Henry Simons, writing at a time when government was small by today's standards, were willing to have government undertake activities that today's liberals would not accept now that government has become so overgrown.

ACTION THROUGH GOVERNMENT
ON PATERNALISTIC GROUNDS

Freedom is a tenable objective only for responsible individuals. We do not believe in freedom for madmen or children. The necessity of drawing a line between responsible individuals and others is inescapable, yet it means that there is an essential ambiguity in our ultimate objective of freedom. Paternalism is inescapable for those whom we designate as not responsible.

The clearest case, perhaps, is that of madmen. We are willing neither to permit them freedom nor to shoot them. It would be nice if we could rely on voluntary activities of individuals to house and care for the madmen. But I think we cannot rule out the possibility that such charitable activities will be inadequate, if only because of the neighborhood effect involved in the fact that I benefit if another man contributes to the care of the insane. For this reason, we may be willing to arrange for their care through government.

Children offer a more difficult case. The ultimate operative unit in our society is the family, not the individual. Yet the acceptance of the family as the unit rests in considerable part on expediency rather than principle. We believe that parents are generally best able to protect their children and to provide for their development into responsible individuals for whom freedom is appropriate. But we do not believe in the freedom of parents to do what they will with other people. The children are responsible individuals in embryo, and a believer in freedom believes in protecting their ultimate rights.

To put this in a different and what may seem a more callous way, children are at one and the same time consumer goods and potentially responsible members of society. The freedom of individuals to use their economic resources as they want includes the freedom to use them to have children — to buy, as it were, the services of children as a particular form of consumption. But once this choice is exercised, the children have a value in and of themselves and have a freedom of their own that is not simply an extension of the freedom of the parents.

The paternalistic ground for governmental activity is in many ways the most troublesome to a liberal; for it involves the acceptance of a principle — that some shall decide for others — which he finds objectionable in most applications and which he rightly regards as a hallmark of his chief intellectual opponents, the proponents of collectivism in one or another of its guises, whether it be communism, socialism, or a welfare state. Yet there is no use pretending that problems are simpler than in fact they are. There is no avoiding the need for some measure of paternalism. As Dicey wrote in 1914 about an act for the protection of mental defectives, "The Mental Deficiency Act is the first step along a path on which no sane man can decline to enter, but which, if too far pursued, will bring statesmen across difficulties hard to meet without considerable interference with individual liberty."[1] There is no formula that can tell us where to stop. We must rely on our fallible judgment and, having reached a judgment, on our ability to persuade our fellow men that it is a correct judgment, or their ability to persuade us to modify our views. We must put our faith, here as elsewhere, in a consensus reached by imperfect and biased men through free discussion and trial and error.

CONCLUSION

A government which maintained law and order, defined property rights, served as a means whereby we could modify property rights and other rules of the economic game, adjudicated disputes about the interpretation of the rules, enforced contracts, promoted competition, provided a monetary framework, engaged in activities to counter technical monopolies and to overcome neighborhood effects widely regarded as sufficiently important to justify government intervention, and which supplemented private charity and the private family in protecting the irresponsible, whether madman or child — such a government would clearly have important functions to perform. The consistent liberal is not an anarchist.

Yet it is also true that such a government would have clearly limited functions and would refrain from a host of activities that are now undertaken by federal and state governments in

[1] A. V. Dicey, *Lectures on the Relation between Law and Public Opinion in England during the Nineteenth Century* (2d. ed.; London: Macmillan & Co., 1914), p. li.

the United States, and their counterparts in other Western countries. Succeeding chapters will deal in some detail with some of these activities, and a few have been discussed above, but it may help to give a sense of proportion about the role that a liberal would assign government simply to list, in closing this chapter, some activities currently undertaken by government in the U.S., that cannot, so far as I can see, validly be justified in terms of the principles outlined above:

1. Parity price support programs for agriculture.

2. Tariffs on imports or restrictions on exports, such as current oil import quotas, sugar quotas, etc.

3. Governmental control of output, such as through the farm program, or through prorationing of oil as is done by the Texas Railroad Commission.

4. Rent control, such as is still practiced in New York, or more general price and wage controls such as were imposed during and just after World War II.

5. Legal minimum wage rates, or legal maximum prices, such as the legal maximum of zero on the rate of interest that can be paid on demand deposits by commercial banks, or the legally fixed maximum rates that can be paid on savings and time deposits.

6. Detailed regulation of industries, such as the regulation of transportation by the Interstate Commerce Commission. This had some justification on technical monopoly grounds when initially introduced for railroads; it has none now for any means of transport. Another example is detailed regulation of banking.

7. A similar example, but one which deserves special mention because of its implicit censorship and violation of free speech, is the control of radio and television by the Federal Communications Commission.

8. Present social security programs, especially the old-age and retirement programs compelling people in effect (*a*) to spend a specified fraction of their income on the purchase of retirement annuity, (*b*) to buy the annuity from a publicly operated enterprise.

9. Licensure provisions in various cities and states which restrict particular enterprises or occupations or professions to people who have a license, where the license is more than a

receipt for a tax which anyone who wishes to enter the activity may pay.

10. So-called "public-housing" and the host of other subsidy programs directed at fostering residential construction such as F.H.A. and V.A. guarantee of mortgage, and the like.

11. Conscription to man the military services in peacetime. The appropriate free market arrangement is volunteer military forces; which is to say, hiring men to serve. There is no justification for not paying whatever price is necessary to attract the required number of men. Present arrangements are inequitable and arbitrary, seriously interfere with the freedom of young men to shape their lives, and probably are even more costly than the market alternative. (Universal military training to provide a reserve for war time is a different problem and may be justified on liberal grounds.)

12. National parks, as noted above.

13. The legal prohibition on the carrying of mail for profit.

14. Publicly owned and operated toll roads, as noted above.

This list is far from comprehensive.

Chapter III

The Control
of Money

"FULL EMPLOYMENT" and "economic growth" have in the past
few decades become primary excuses for widening the extent of
government intervention in economic affairs. A private free-
enterprise economy, it is said, is inherently unstable. Left to itself,
it will produce recurrent cycles of boom and bust. The government must therefore step in to keep things on an even keel. These
arguments were particularly potent during and after the Great
Depression of the 1930's, and were a major element giving rise to
the New Deal in this country and comparable extensions of governmental intervention in others. More recently, "economic
growth" has become the more popular rallying call. Government must, it is argued, see to it that the economy expands to
provide the wherewithal for the cold war and demonstrate to

the uncommitted nations of the world that a democracy can grow more rapidly than a communist state.

These arguments are thoroughly misleading. The fact is that the Great Depression, like most other periods of severe unemployment, was produced by government mismanagement rather than by any inherent instability of the private economy. A governmentally established agency — the Federal Reserve System — had been assigned responsibility for monetary policy. In 1930 and 1931, it exercised this responsibility so ineptly as to convert what otherwise would have been a moderate contraction into a major catastrophe (see further discussion, pages 45–50, below). Similarly today, governmental measures constitute the major impediments to economic growth in the United States. Tariffs and other restrictions on international trade, high tax burdens and a complex and inequitable tax structure, regulatory commissions, government price and wage fixing, and a host of other measures give individuals an incentive to misuse and misdirect resources, and distort the investment of new savings. What we urgently need, for both economic stability and growth, is a reduction of government intervention not an increase.

Such a reduction would still leave an important role for government in these areas. It is desirable that we use government to provide a stable monetary framework for a free economy — this is part of the function of providing a stable legal framework. It is desirable too that we use government to provide a general legal and economic framework that will enable individuals to produce growth in the economy, if that is in accord with their values.

The major areas of governmental policy that are relevant to economic stability are monetary policy and fiscal or budgetary policy. This chapter discusses domestic monetary policy, the next, international monetary arrangements, and chapter v, fiscal or budgetary policy.

Our task in this and the following chapter is to steer a course between two views, neither of which is acceptable though both have their attractions. The Scylla is the belief that a purely automatic gold standard is both feasible and desirable and would resolve all the problems of fostering economic co-operation among individuals and nations in a stable environment. The Charybdis is the belief that the need to adapt to unforeseen circumstances requires the assignment of wide discretionary powers to a group of technicians, gathered together in an "independent" central bank, or in some bureaucratic body. Neither has proved a satisfactory solution in the past; and neither is likely to in the future.

A liberal is fundamentally fearful of concentrated power. His objective is to preserve the maximum degree of freedom for each individual separately that is compatible with one man's freedom not interfering with other men's freedom. He believes that this objective requires that power be dispersed. He is suspicious of assigning to government any functions that can be performed through the market, both because this substitutes coercion for voluntary co-operation in the area in question and because, by giving government an increased role, it threatens freedom in other areas.

The need for the dispersal of power raises an especially difficult problem in the field of money. There is widespread agreement that government must have some responsibility for monetary matters. There is also widespread recognition that control over money can be a potent tool for controlling and shaping the economy. Its potency is dramatized in Lenin's famous dictum that the most effective way to destroy a society is to destroy its money. It is exemplified in more pedestrian fashion by the extent to which control of money has, from time immemorial, enabled sovereigns to exact heavy taxes from the populace at large, very often without the explicit agreement of the legislature when there has been one. This has been true from early times when monarchs clipped coins and adopted similar expedients to the present with our more sophisticated modern techniques for turning the printing press or simply altering book entries. The problem is to establish institutional arrangements that will enable government to exercise responsibility for money, yet at the same time limit the power thereby given to government and prevent this power from being used in ways that will tend to weaken rather than strengthen a free society.

A COMMODITY STANDARD

Historically, the device that has evolved most frequently in many different places and over the course of centuries is a commodity standard; i.e., the use as money of some physical commodity such as gold or silver, brass or tin, cigarettes or cognac, or various other goods. If money consisted wholly of a physical commodity of this type, there would be, in principle, no need for control by the government at all. The amount of money in society would depend on the cost of producing the monetary commodity rather than other things. Changes in the amount of money would depend on changes in the technical conditions of producing the monetary commodity and on changes in the demand for money. This is an ideal that animates many believers in an automatic gold standard.

Actual commodity standards have deviated very far from this simple pattern which requires no governmental intervention. Historically, a commodity standard — such as a gold standard or a silver standard — has been accompanied by the development of fiduciary money of one kind or another, ostensibly convertible into the monetary commodity on fixed terms. There was a very good reason for this development. The fundamental defect of a commodity standard, from the point of view of the society as a whole, is that it requires the use of real resources to add to the stock of money. People must work hard to dig gold out of the ground in South Africa — in order to rebury it in Fort Knox or some similar place. The necessity of using real resources for the operation of a commodity standard establishes a strong incentive for people to find ways to achieve the same result without employing these resources. If people will accept as money pieces of paper on which is printed "I promise to pay ——— units of the commodity standard," these pieces of paper can perform the same function as the physical pieces of gold or silver, and they require very much less in resources to produce. This point, which I have discussed at somewhat greater length elsewhere,[1] seems to me the fundamental difficulty with a commodity standard.

If an automatic commodity standard were feasible, it would provide an excellent solution to the liberal's dilemma: a stable

[1] *A Program for Monetary Stability* (New York: Fordham University Press, 1959) pp. 4–8.

monetary framework without the danger of the irresponsible exercise of monetary powers. If, for example, an honest-to-goodness gold standard, in which 100 per cent of the money in a country consisted literally of gold, were widely backed by the public at large, imbued with the mythology of a gold standard and with the belief that it is immoral and improper for government to interfere with its operation, it would provide an effective guarantee against governmental tinkering with the currency and against irresponsible monetary action. Under such a standard, any monetary powers of government would be very minor in scope. But, as just noted, such an automatic system has historically never proved feasible. It has always tended to develop in the direction of a mixed system containing fiduciary elements such as bank notes and deposits, or government notes in addition to the monetary commodity. And once fiduciary elements have been introduced, it has proved difficult to avoid governmental control over them, even when they were initially issued by private individuals. The reason is basically the difficulty of preventing counterfeiting or its economic equivalent. Fiduciary money is a contract to pay standard money. It so happens that there tends to be a long interval between the making of such a contract and its realization. This enhances the difficulty of enforcing the contract and hence also the temptation to issue fraudulent contracts. In addition, once fiduciary elements have been introduced, the temptation for government itself to issue fiduciary money is almost irresistible. In practice, therefore, commodity standards have tended to become mixed standards involving extensive intervention by the state.

It should be noted that despite the great amount of talk by many people in favor of the gold standard, almost no one today literally desires an honest-to-goodness, full gold standard. People who say they want a gold standard are almost invariably talking about the present kind of standard, or the kind of standard that was maintained in the 1930's; a gold standard managed by a central bank or other governmental bureau, which holds a small amount of gold as "backing" — to use that very misleading term — for fiduciary money. Some do go so far as to favor the kind of standard maintained in the 1920's, in which there was literal circulation of gold or gold certificates as hand-to-hand currency—a gold-coin standard—but even they favor the co-existence with gold of governmental fiduciary currency plus deposits issued by banks holding fractional reserves in either gold or fiduciary currency. Even during the so-called great days of the gold standard in the nineteenth century, when the Bank of England was supposedly running the gold standard skilfully, the monetary system was far from a fully automatic gold standard. Even then it was a highly managed standard. And certainly the situation is now more extreme as a result of the adoption by country after country of the view that government has responsibility for "full employment."

My conclusion is that an automatic commodity standard is neither a feasible nor a desirable solution to the problem of establishing monetary arrangements for a free society. It is not desirable because it would involve a large cost in the form of resources used to produce the monetary commodity. It is not feasible because the mythology and beliefs required to make it effective do not exist.

This conclusion is supported not only by the general historical evidence referred to but also by the specific experience of the United States. From 1879, when the United States resumed gold payments after the Civil War, to 1913, the United States was on a gold standard. Though closer to a thoroughly automatic gold standard than anything we have had since the end of World War I, the gold standard was still far from a 100 per cent gold standard. There were government issues of paper money, and private banks issued most of the effective circulating medium of the country in the form of deposits; the banks were closely regulated in their operations by governmental agencies—national banks by the Comptroller of the Currency, state banks by state banking authorities. Gold, whether held by the Treasury, by banks, or directly by individuals as coins or gold certificates, accounted for between 10 per cent and 20 per cent of the money stock, the exact percentage varying from year to year. The remaining 80 per cent to 90 per cent consisted of silver, fiduciary currency, and bank deposits not matched by gold reserves.

In retrospect, the system may seem to us to have worked reasonably well. To Americans of the time, it clearly did not. The agitation over silver in the 1880's, culminating in Bryan's Cross of Gold speech which set the tone for the 1896 election, was one sign of dissatisfaction. In turn, the agitation was largely responsible for the severely depressed years in the early 1890's. The agitation led to widespread fears that the United States would go off gold and that hence the dollar would lose value in terms of foreign currencies. This led to a flight from the dollar and a capital outflow that forced deflation at home.

Successive financial crises, in 1873, 1884, 1890, and 1893 produced a widespread demand for banking reform on the part of the business and banking community. The panic of 1907, involving the concerted refusal by banks to convert deposits into currency on demand, finally crystallized the feeling of dissatisfaction with the financial system into an urgent demand for governmental action. A National Monetary Commission was established by Congress, and its recommendations, reported in 1910, were embodied in the Federal Reserve Act passed in 1913. Reforms along the lines of the Federal Reserve Act had the backing of every section of the community, from the working classes to the bankers, and of both political parties. The chairman of the National Monetary Commission was a Republican, Nelson W. Aldrich; the Senator mainly responsible for the Federal Reserve Act was a Democrat, Carter W. Glass.

The change in monetary arrangements introduced by the Federal Reserve Act turned out in practice to be far more drastic than was intended by its authors or its supporters. At the time the Act was passed, a gold standard reigned supreme throughout the world — not a fully automatic gold standard but something far closer to that ideal than anything we have experienced since. It was taken for granted that it would continue to do so and thus narrowly limit the powers of the Federal Reserve System. No sooner was the Act passed than World War I broke out. There was a large-scale abandonment of the gold standard. By the end of the war, the Reserve System was no longer a minor adjunct to the gold standard designed to insure the convertibility of one form of money into others and to regulate and supervise banks. It had become a powerful discretionary authority able to determine the quantity of money in the United States and to affect international financial conditions throughout the world.

A DISCRETIONARY MONETARY AUTHORITY

The establishment of the Federal Reserve System was the most notable change in United States monetary institutions since at least the Civil War National Banking Act. For the first time since the expiration of the charter of the Second Bank of the United States in 1836, it established a separate official body charged with explicit responsibility for monetary conditions, and supposedly clothed with adequate power to achieve monetary stability or, at least, to prevent pronounced instability. It is therefore instructive to compare experience as a whole before and after its establishment — say, from just after the Civil War to 1914 and from 1914 to date, to take two periods of equal length.

The second period was clearly the more unstable economically, whether instability is measured by the fluctuations in the stock of money, in prices, or in output. Partly, the greater instability reflects the effect of two world wars during the second period; these would clearly have been a source of instability whatever our monetary system. But even if the war and immediate postwar years are omitted, and we consider only the peacetime years from, say, 1920 through 1939, and 1947 to date, the result is the same. The stock of money, prices, and output was decidedly more unstable after the establishment of the Reserve System than before. The most dramatic period of instability in output was of course the period between the two wars which includes the severe contractions of 1920–21, 1929–33, and 1937–38. No other twenty-year period in American history contains as many as three such severe contractions.

This crude comparison does not of course prove that the Federal Reserve System failed to contribute to monetary stability. Perhaps the problems that the System had to handle were more severe than those that impinged on the earlier monetary structure. Perhaps those problems would have produced an even greater degree of monetary instability under the earlier arrangements. But the crude comparison should at least give the reader pause before he takes for granted, as is so often done, that an agency as long established, as powerful, as pervasive as the Federal Reserve System is performing a necessary and desirable function and is contributing to the attainment of the objectives for which it was established.

I am myself persuaded, on the basis of extensive study of the historical evidence, that the difference in economic stability revealed by the crude comparison is in fact attributable to the difference in monetary institutions. This evidence persuades me that at least a third of the price rise during and just after World War I is attributable to the establishment of the Federal Reserve System and would not have occurred if the earlier banking system had been retained; that the severity of each of the major contractions — 1920–21, 1929–33, and 1937–38 — is directly attributable to acts of commission and omission by the Reserve authorities and would not have occurred under earlier monetary and banking arrangements. There might well have been recessions on these or other occasions, but it is highly unlikely that any would have developed into a major contraction.

I clearly cannot present this evidence here.[2] However, in view of the importance which the Great Depression of 1929–33 played in forming — or, I would say, deforming — general attitudes toward the role of government in economic affairs, it may be worth indicating more fully for this episode the kind of interpretation suggested by the evidence.

Because of its dramatic character, the stock market crash in October, 1929, which terminated the bull market of 1928 and 1929 is often regarded as both the start and the major proximate cause of the Great Depression. Neither is correct. The peak of business was reached in mid-1929, some months prior to the crash. The peak may well have come as early as it did partly as a result of relatively tight money conditions imposed by the Federal Reserve System in an attempt to curb "speculation" — in this indirect way, the stock market may have played a role in bringing about the contraction. The stock market crash in turn undoubtedly had some indirect effects on business confidence

[2] See my *A Program for Monetary Stability* and Milton Friedman and Anna J. Schwartz, *A Monetary History of the United States, 1867–1960* (forthcoming by Princeton University Press for the National Bureau of Economic Research).

and on the willingness of individuals to spend which exerted a depressing influence on the course of business. But by themselves, these effects could not have produced a collapse in economic activity. At most, they would have made the contraction somewhat longer and more severe than the usual mild recessions that have punctuated American economic growth throughout our history; they would not have made it the catastrophe it was.

For something like the first year, the contraction showed none of those special features that were to dominate its later course. The economic decline was more severe than during the first year of most contractions, possibly in response to the stock market crash plus the unusually tight monetary conditions that had been maintained since mid-1928. But it showed no qualitatively different characteristics, no signs of degenerating into a major catastrophe. Except on naïve *post hoc ergo propter hoc* reasoning, there is nothing in the economic situation as it stood in, say, September or October, 1930 that made the continued and drastic decline of the following years inevitable or even highly probable. In retrospect, it is clear that the Reserve System should already have been behaving differently than it did, that it should not have allowed the money stock to decline by nearly 3 per cent from August 1929 to October 1930 — a larger decline than during the whole of all but the most severe prior contractions. Though this was a mistake, it was perhaps excusable, and certainly not critical.

The character of the contraction changed drastically in November 1930, when a series of bank failures led to widespread runs on banks, which is to say attempts by depositors to convert deposits into currency. The contagion spread from one part of the country to another and reached a climax with the failure on December 11, 1930 of the Bank of the United States. This failure was critical not only because the Bank was one of the largest in the country, with over $200 million in deposits, but also because, though an ordinary commercial bank, its name had led many both at home and even more abroad to regard it as somehow an official bank.

Prior to October, 1930, there had been no sign of a liquidity crisis, or any loss of confidence in banks. From this time on, the economy was plagued by recurrent liquidity crises. A wave of bank failures would taper down a while, and then start up again as a few dramatic failures or other events produced a new loss of confidence in the banking system and a new series of runs on banks. These were important not only or even primarily because of the failures of the banks but because of their effect on the money stock.

In a fractional reserve banking system like ours, a bank does not of course have a dollar of currency (or its equivalent) for a dollar of deposits. That is why "deposits" is such a misleading term. When you deposit a dollar of cash in a bank, the bank may add fifteen or twenty cents to its cash; the rest it will lend out through another window. The borrower may in turn redeposit it, in this or another bank, and the process is repeated. The result is that for every dollar of cash owned by banks, they owe several dollars of deposits. The total stock of money — cash plus deposits — for a given amount of cash is therefore higher the larger the fraction of its money the public is willing to hold as deposits. Any widespread attempt on the part of depositors to "get their money" must therefore mean a decline in the total amount of money unless there is some way in which additional cash can be created and some way for banks to get it. Otherwise, one bank, in trying to satisfy its depositors, will put pressure on other banks by calling loans or selling investments or withdrawing its deposits and these other banks in turn will put pressure on still others. The vicious cycle, if allowed to proceed, grows on itself as the attempt of banks to get cash forces down the prices of securities, renders banks insolvent that would otherwise have been entirely sound, shakes the confidence of depositors, and starts the cycle over again.

This was precisely the kind of a situation that had led to a banking panic under the pre-Federal-Reserve banking system, and to a concerted suspension of the convertibility of deposits into currency, as in 1907. Such a suspension was a drastic step and for a short while made matters worse. But it was also a therapeutic measure. It cut short the vicious cycle by preventing the spread of the contagion, by keeping the failure of a few banks from producing pressure on other banks and leading to the failure of otherwise sound banks. In a few weeks or months, when the situation had stabilized, the suspension could be lifted, and recovery begin without monetary contraction.

As we have seen, one of the major reasons for establishing the Federal Reserve System was to deal with such a situation. It was given the power to create more cash if a widespread demand should arise on the part of the public for currency instead of deposits, and was given the means to make the cash available to banks on the security of the bank's assets. In this way, it was expected that any threatened panic could be averted, that there would be no need for suspension of convertibility of deposits into currency, and that the depressing effects of monetary crises could be entirely avoided.

The first need for these powers and hence the first test of their efficacy came in November and December of 1930 as a result of the string of bank closings already described. The Reserve System failed the test miserably. It did little or nothing to provide the banking system with liquidity, apparently regarding the bank closings as calling for no special action. It is worth emphasizing, however, that the System's failure was a failure of will, not of power. On this occasion, as on the later ones that followed, the System had ample power to provide the banks with the cash their depositors were demanding. Had this been done, the bank closings would have been cut short and the monetary debacle averted.

The initial wave of bank failures died down and in early 1931 there were signs of returning confidence. The Reserve System took advantage of the opportunity to reduce its own credit outstanding—which is to say, it offset the naturally expansionary forces by engaging in mild deflationary action. Even so, there were clear signs of improvement not only in the monetary sector but also in other economic activities. The figures for the first four or five months of 1931, if examined without reference to what actually followed, have all the earmarks of the bottom of a cycle and the beginning of revival.

The tentative revival was however short-lived. Renewed bank failures started another series of runs and again set in train a renewed decline in the stock of money. Again, the Reserve System stood idly by. In the face of an unprecedented liquidation of the commercial banking system, the books of the "lender of last resort" show a *decline* in the amount of credit it made available to its member banks.

In September 1931, Britain went off the gold standard. This act was preceded and followed by gold withdrawals from the United States. Although gold had been flowing into the United States in the prior two years, and the U.S. gold stock and the Federal Reserve gold reserve ratio were at an all time high, the Reserve System reacted vigorously and promptly to the external drain as it had not to the previous internal drain. It did so in a manner that was certain to intensify the internal financial difficulties. After more than two years of severe economic contraction, the System raised the discount rate — the rate of interest at which it stood ready to lend to member banks — more sharply than it has within so brief a period in its whole history before or since. The measure arrested the gold drain. It was also accompanied by a spectacular increase in bank failures and runs on banks. In the six months from August 1931 through January 1932, roughly one out of ten banks in existence suspended operations and total deposits in commercial banks fell by 15 per cent.

A temporary reversal of policy in 1932 involving the purchase of $1 billion of government bonds slowed down the rate of decline. Had this measure been taken in 1931, it would almost surely have been sufficient to prevent the debacle just described. By 1932, it was too late to be more than a palliative and, when the System relapsed into passivity, the temporary improvement was followed by a renewed collapse terminating in the Banking Holiday of 1933 — when every bank in the United States was officially closed for over a week. A system established in large part to prevent a temporary suspension of convertibility of deposits into currency — a measure that had formerly prevented banks from failing — first let nearly a third of the banks of the country go out of existence and then welcomed a suspension of convertibility that was incomparably more sweeping and severe than any earlier suspension. Yet so great is the capacity for self-justification that the Federal Reserve Board could write in its annual report for 1933, "The ability of the Federal Reserve Banks to meet enormous demands for currency during the crisis demonstrated the effectiveness of the country's currency system under the Federal Reserve Act. . . . It is difficult to say what the course of the depression would have been had the Federal Reserve System not pursued a policy of liberal open market purchases."

All told, from July 1929 to March 1933, the money stock in the United States fell by one-third, and over two-thirds of the decline came after England's departure from the gold standard. Had the money stock been kept from declining, as it clearly could and should have been, the contraction would have been both shorter and far milder. It might still have been relatively severe by historical standards. But it is literally inconceivable that money income could have declined by over one-half and prices by over one-third in the course of four years if there had been no decline in the stock of money. I know of no severe depression in any country or any time that was not accompanied by a sharp decline in the stock of money and equally of no sharp decline in the stock of money that was not accompanied by a severe depression.

The Great Depression in the United States, far from being a sign of the inherent instability of the private enterprise system, is a testament to how much harm can be done by mistakes on the part of a few men when they wield vast power over the monetary system of a country.

It may be that these mistakes were excusable on the basis of the knowledge available to men at the time — though I happen to think not. But that is really beside the point. Any system which gives so much power and so much discretion to a few men that mistakes — excusable or not — can have such far-reaching effects is a bad system. It is a bad system to believers in freedom just because it gives a few men such power without any effective check by the body politic — this is the key political argument against an "independent" central bank. But it is a bad system even to those who set security higher than freedom. Mistakes, excusable or not, cannot be avoided in a system which disperses responsibility yet gives a few men great power, and which thereby makes important policy actions highly dependent on accidents of personality. This is the key technical argument against an "independent" bank. To paraphrase Clemenceau, money is much too serious a matter to be left to the Central Bankers.

If we can achieve our objectives neither by relying on the working of a thoroughly automatic gold standard nor by giving wide discretion to independent authorities, how else can we establish a monetary system that is stable and at the same time free from irresponsible governmental tinkering, a system that will provide the necessary monetary framework for a free enterprise economy yet be incapable of being used as a source of power to threaten economic and political freedom?

The only way that has yet been suggested that offers promise is to try to achieve a government of law instead of men by legislating rules for the conduct of monetary policy that will have the effect of enabling the public to exercise control over monetary policy through its political authorities, while at the same time it will prevent monetary policy from being subject to the day-by-day whim of political authorities.

The issue of legislating rules for monetary policy has much in common with a topic that seems at first altogether different, namely, the argument for the first amendment to the Constitution. Whenever anyone suggests the desirability of a legislative rule for control over money, the stereotyped answer is that it makes little sense to tie the monetary authority's hands in this way because the authority, if it wants to, can always do of its own volition what the rule would require it to do, and in addition has other alternatives, hence "surely," it is said, it can do better than the rule. An alternative version of the same argument applies it to the legislature. If the legislature is willing to adopt the rule, it is said, surely it will also be willing to legislate the "right" policy in each specific case. How then, it is said, does the adoption of the rule provide any protection against irresponsible political action?

The same argument could apply with only minor verbal changes to the first amendment to the Constitution and, equally, to the entire Bill of Rights. Is it not absurd, one might say, to have a standard proscription of interference with free speech?

Why not take up each case separately and treat it on its own merits? Is this not the counterpart to the usual argument in monetary policy that it is undesirable to bind the hands of the monetary authority in advance; that it should be left free to treat each case on its merits as it comes up? Why is not the argument equally valid for speech? One man wants to stand up on a street corner and advocate birth control; another, communism; a third, vegetarianism, and so on, *ad infinitum*. Why not enact a law affirming or denying to each the right to spread his particular views? Or, alternatively, why not give the power to decide the issue to an administrative agency? It is immediately clear that if we were to take each case up as it came, a majority would almost surely vote to deny free speech in most cases and perhaps even in every case taken separately. A vote on whether Mr. X should spread birth control propaganda would almost surely yield a majority saying no; and so would one on communism. The vegetarian might perhaps get by though even that is by no means a foregone conclusion.

But now suppose all these cases were grouped together in one bundle, and the populace at large were asked to vote for them as a whole; to vote whether free speech should be denied in all cases or permitted in all alike. It is perfectly conceivable, and I would say, highly probable, that an overwhelming majority would vote for free speech; that, acting on the bundle as a whole, the people would vote exactly the opposite to the way they would have voted on each case separately. Why? One reason is that each person feels much more strongly about being deprived of his right to free speech when he is in a minority than he feels about depriving somebody else of the right to free speech when he is in the majority. In consequence, when he votes on the bundle as a whole, he gives much more weight to the infrequent denial of free speech to himself when he is in the minority than to the frequent denial of free speech to others.

Another reason, and one that is more directly relevant to monetary policy, is that if the bundle is viewed as a whole, it becomes clear that the policy followed has cumulative effects that tend neither to be recognized nor taken into account when each case is voted on separately. When a vote is taken on whether Mr. Jones can speak on the corner, it cannot allow for the favorable effects of an announced general policy of free speech. It cannot allow for the fact that a society in which people are not free to speak on the corner without special legislation will be a society in which the development of new ideas, experimentation, change, and the like will all be hampered in a great variety of ways that are obvious to all, thanks to our good fortune of having lived in a society which did adopt the self-denying ordinance of not considering each case of speech separately.

Exactly the same considerations apply in the monetary area. If each case is considered on its merits, the wrong decision is likely to be made in a large fraction of cases because the decision-makers are examining only a limited area and not taking into account the cumulative consequences of the policy as a whole. On the other hand, if a general rule is adopted for a group of cases as a bundle, the existence of that rule has favorable effects on people's attitudes and beliefs and expectations that would not follow even from the discretionary adoption of precisely the same policy on a series of separate occasions.

If a rule is to be legislated, what rule should it be? The rule that has most frequently been suggested by people of a generally liberal persuasion is a price level rule; namely, a legislative directive to the monetary authorities that they maintain a stable price level. I think this is the wrong kind of a rule. It is the wrong kind of a rule because it is in terms of objectives that the monetary authorities do not have the clear and direct power to achieve by their own actions. It consequently raises the problem of dispersing responsibilities and leaving the authorities too much leeway. There is unquestionably a close connection between monetary actions and the price level. But the connection is not so close, so invariable, or so direct that the objective of achieving a stable price level is an appropriate guide to the day-to-day activities of the authorities.

The issue what rule to adopt is one that I have considered at some length elsewhere.[3] Accordingly, I will limit myself here

[3] *A Program for Monetary Stability, op. cit.,* pp. 77–99.

to stating my conclusion. In the present state of our knowledge, it seems to me desirable to state the rule in terms of the behavior of the stock of money. My choice at the moment would be a legislated rule instructing the monetary authority to achieve a specified rate of growth in the stock of money. For this purpose, I would define the stock of money as including currency outside commercial banks plus all deposits of commercial banks. I would specify that the Reserve System shall see to it that the total stock of money so defined rises month by month, and indeed, so far as possible, day by day, at an annual rate of X per cent, where X is some number between 3 and 5. The precise definition of money adopted, or the precise rate of growth chosen, makes far less difference than the definite choice of a particular definition and a particular rate of growth.

As matters now stand, while this rule would drastically curtail the discretionary power of the monetary authorities, it would still leave an undesirable amount of discretion in the hands of Federal Reserve and Treasury authorities with respect to how to achieve the specified rate of growth in the money stock, debt management, banking supervision, and the like. Further banking and fiscal reforms, which I have spelled out in detail elsewhere, are both feasible and desirable. They would have the effect of eliminating present governmental intervention into lending and investing activity and of converting governmental financing operations from a perpetual source of instability and uncertainty into a reasonably regular and predictable activity. But, though important, these further reforms are far less basic than the adoption of a rule to limit the discretion of the monetary authorities with respect to the stock of money.

I should like to emphasize that I do not regard my particular proposal as a be-all and end-all of monetary management, as a rule which is somehow to be written in tablets of stone and enshrined for all future time. It seems to me to be the rule that offers the greatest promise of achieving a reasonable degree of monetary stability in the light of our present knowledge. I would hope that as we operated with it, as we learned more about monetary matters, we might be able to devise still better rules, which would achieve still better results. Such a rule seems to me the only feasible device currently available for converting monetary policy into a pillar of a free society rather than a threat to its foundations.

Chapter IV

International Financial and
Trade Arrangements

T HE PROBLEM of international monetary arrangements is the relation among different national currencies: the terms and conditions under which individuals are able to convert U.S. dollars to pounds sterling, Canadian dollars to U.S. dollars, and so on. This problem is closely connected with the control of money discussed in the preceding chapter. It is connected also with governmental policies about international trade, since control over international trade is one technique for affecting international payments.

THE IMPORTANCE OF INTERNATIONAL
MONETARY ARRANGEMENTS FOR ECONOMIC FREEDOM

Despite its technical character and forbidding complexity, the subject of international monetary arrangements is one that a liberal cannot afford to neglect. It is not too much to say that the most serious short-run threat to economic freedom in the United States today — aside, of course, from the outbreak of World War III — is that we shall be led to adopt far-reaching economic controls in order to "solve" balance of payments problems. Interferences with international trade appear innocuous; they can get the support of people who are otherwise apprehensive of interference by government into economic affairs; many a business man even regards them as part of the "American Way of Life"; yet there are few interferences which are capable of spreading so far and ultimately being so destructive of free enterprise. There is much experience to suggest that the most effective way to convert a market economy into an authoritarian economic society is to start by imposing direct controls on foreign exchange. This one step leads inevitably to the rationing of imports, to control over domestic production that uses imported products or that produces substitutes for imports, and so on in a never-ending spiral. Yet even so generally staunch a champion of free enterprise as Senator Barry Goldwater has at times been led, when discussing the so-called "gold flow," to suggest that restrictions on transactions in foreign exchange may be necessary as a "cure." This "cure" would be vastly worse than the disease.

There is seldom anything truly new under the sun in economic policy, where the allegedly new generally turns out to be the discard of a prior century in flimsy disguise. Unless I am mistaken, however, full-fledged exchange controls and so-called "inconvertibility of currencies" are an exception and their origin reveals their authoritarian promise. To the best of my knowledge they were invented by Hjalmar Schacht in the early years of the Nazi regime. On many occasions in the past, of course, currencies have been described as inconvertible. But what the word then meant was that the government of the day was unwilling or unable to convert paper currency into gold or silver, or whatever the monetary commodity was, at the legally stipulated rate. It seldom meant that a country prohibited its citizens or residents from trading pieces of paper promising to pay specified sums in the monetary unit of that country for corresponding pieces of paper expressed in the

monetary unit of another country—or for that matter for coin
or bullion. During the Civil War in the United States and for
a decade and a half thereafter, for example, U.S. currency was
inconvertible in the sense that the holder of a greenback could
not turn it in to the Treasury and get a fixed amount of gold
for it. But throughout the period he was free to buy gold at
the market price or to buy and sell British pounds for U.S.
greenbacks at any price mutually agreeable to the two parties.

In the United States, the dollar has been inconvertible in the
older sense ever since 1933. It has been illegal for American
citizens to hold gold or to buy and sell gold. The dollar has
not been inconvertible in the newer sense. But unfortunately
we seem to be adopting policies that are highly likely, sooner
or later, to drive us in that direction.

THE ROLE OF GOLD IN THE U.S. MONETARY SYSTEM

Only a cultural lag leads us still to think of gold as the central element in our monetary system. A more accurate descrip-
tion of the role of gold in U.S. policy is that it is primarily a
commodity whose price is supported, like wheat or other agricultural products. Our price-support program for gold differs
in three important respects from our price-support program for
wheat: first, we pay the support price to foreign as well as
domestic producers; second, we sell freely at the support price
only to foreign purchasers and not to domestic; third, and this
is the one important relic of the monetary role of gold, the
Treasury is authorized to create money to pay for gold it buys
—to print paper money as it were—so that expenditures for
the purchase of gold do not appear in the budget and the sums
required need not be explicitly appropriated by Congress; similarly, when the Treasury sells gold, the books show simply a
reduction in gold certificates, and not a receipt that enters into
the budget.

When the price of gold was first set at its present level of
$35 an ounce in 1934, this price was well above the free market
price of gold. In consequence, gold flooded the United States,
our gold stock tripled in six years, and we came to hold well
over half the world's gold stock. We accumulated a "surplus"

of gold for the same reason we accumulated a "surplus" of wheat — because the government offered to pay a higher price than the market price. More recently, the situation has changed. While the legally fixed price of gold has remained $35, prices of other goods have doubled or tripled. Hence $35 is now less than what the free market price would be.[1] As a result, we now face a "shortage" rather than a "surplus" for precisely the same reason that rent ceilings inevitably produce a "shortage" of housing — because the government is trying to hold the price of gold below the market price.

The legal price of gold would long since have been raised — as wheat prices have been raised from time to time — except for the accident that the major producers of gold, and hence the major beneficiaries from a rise in its price, are Soviet Russia and South Africa, the two countries with whom the United States has least political sympathy.

Governmental control of the price of gold, no less than the control of any other price, is inconsistent with a free economy. Such a pseudo gold standard must be distinguished sharply from the use of gold as money under a real gold standard which is entirely consistent with a free economy though it may not be feasible. Even more than the price fixing itself, the associated measures taken in 1933 and 1934 by the Roosevelt administration when it raised the price of gold represented a fundamental departure from liberal principles and established precedents that have returned to plague the free world. I refer to the nationalization of the gold stock, the prohibition of private possession of gold for monetary purposes, and the abrogation of gold clauses in public and private contracts.

In 1933 and early 1934, private holders of gold were required by law to turn over their gold to the federal government. They were compensated at a price equal to the prior legal price, which was at the time decidedly below the market price. To make this requirement effective, private ownership of gold within the U.S. was made illegal except for use in the arts. One can hardly imagine a measure more destructive of the princi-

---

[1] A warning is in order that this is a subtle point that depends on what is held constant in estimating the free market price, particularly with respect to gold's monetary role.

ples of private property on which a free enterprise society rests. There is no difference in principle between this nationalization of gold at an artificially low price and Fidel Castro's nationalization of land and factories at an artificially low price. On what grounds of principle can the U.S. object to the one after having itself engaged in the other? Yet so great is the blindness of some supporters of free enterprise with respect to anything touching gold that in 1960 Henry Alexander, head of the Morgan Guaranty Trust Company, successor to J. P. Morgan and Company, proposed that the prohibition against the private ownership of gold by U.S. citizens be extended to cover gold held abroad! And his proposal was adopted by President Eisenhower with hardly a protest from the banking community.

Though rationalized in terms of "conserving" gold for monetary use, prohibition of private ownership of gold was not enacted for any such monetary purpose, whether itself good or bad. The nationalization of gold was enacted to enable the government to reap the whole of the "paper" profit from the rise in the price of gold—or perhaps, to prevent private individuals from benefiting.

The abrogation of the gold clauses had a similar purpose. And this too was a measure destructive of the basic principles of free enterprise. Contracts entered into in good faith and with full knowledge on the part of both parties to them were declared invalid for the benefit of one of the parties!

CURRENT PAYMENTS AND CAPITAL FLIGHT

In discussing international monetary relations on a more general level, it is necessary to distinguish two rather different problems: the balance of payments, and the danger of a run on gold. The difference between the problems can be illustrated most simply by considering the analogy of an ordinary commercial bank. The bank must so arrange its affairs that it takes in as service charges, interest on loans, and so on a large enough sum to enable it to pay its expenses—wages and salaries, interest on borrowed funds, cost of supplies, returns to stockholders, and so on. It must strive, that is, for a healthy income account. But a bank which is in good shape on its income account may nonetheless experience serious trouble if for any reason its depositors should lose confidence in it and suddenly demand their deposits en masse. Many a sound bank was forced to close its doors because of such a run on it during the liquidity crises described in the preceding chapter.

These two problems are not of course unrelated. One important reason why a bank's depositors may lose confidence in it is because the bank is experiencing losses on income account. Yet the two problems are also very different. For one thing, problems on income account are generally slow to arise and considerable time is available to solve them. They seldom come as sudden surprises. A run, on the other hand, may arise suddenly and unpredictably out of thin air.

The situation of the U.S. is precisely parallel. Residents of the United States and the U.S. government itself are seeking to buy foreign currencies with dollars in order to purchase goods and services in other countries, to invest in foreign enterprises, to pay interest on debts, to repay loans, or to give gifts to others, whether private or public. At the same time, foreigners are seeking to acquire dollars with foreign currencies for corresponding purposes. After the event, the number of dollars spent for foreign currency will precisely equal the number of dollars purchased with foreign currency — just as the number of pairs of shoes sold is precisely equal to the number bought. Arithmetic is arithmetic and one man's purchase is another man's sale. But there is nothing to assure that, *at any given price of foreign currency in terms of dollars*, the number of dollars that some want to spend will equal the number others want to buy — just as there is nothing to assure that *at any given price of shoes* the number of pairs of shoes people want to buy is exactly equal to the number of pairs other people want to sell. The *ex post* equality reflects some mechanism that eliminates any *ex ante* discrepancy. The problem of achieving an appropriate mechanism for this purpose is the counterpart of the bank's problem on income account.

In addition, the United States has a problem like the bank's of avoiding a run. The U.S. is committed to sell gold to foreign central banks and governments at $35 an ounce. Foreign central banks, governments, and residents hold large funds in the United States in the form of deposit accounts or U.S. securities that can be readily sold for dollars. At any time, the holders of these balances can start a run on the U.S. Treasury by trying to convert their dollar balances into gold. This is precisely what happened in the fall of 1960, and what is very likely to happen again at some unpredictable date in the future (perhaps before this is printed).

The two problems are related in two ways. In the first place, as for a bank, income account difficulties are a major source of loss of confidence in the ability of the U.S. to honor its promise to sell gold at $35 an ounce. The fact that the U.S. has in effect been having to borrow abroad in order to achieve balance on current account is a major reason why holders of dollars are interested in converting them into gold or other currencies. In the second place, the fixed price of gold is the device we have adopted for pegging another set of prices — the price of the dollar in terms of foreign currencies — and flows of gold are the device we have adopted for resolving *ex ante* discrepancies in the balance of payments.

ALTERNATIVE MECHANISMS FOR
ACHIEVING BALANCE IN FOREIGN PAYMENTS

We can get more light on both of these relations by considering what alternative mechanisms are available for achieving balance in payments — the first and in many ways the more fundamental of the two problems.

Suppose that the U.S. is roughly in balance in its international payments and that something comes along which alters the situation by, let us say, reducing the number of dollars that foreigners want to buy compared to the number that U.S. residents want to sell; or, looking at it from the other side, increasing the amount of foreign currency that holders of dollars want to buy compared to the amount that holders of foreign currency want to sell for dollars. That is, something threatens to produce a "deficit" in U.S. payments. This might result from increased efficiency in production abroad or decreased efficiency at home, increased foreign aid expenditures by the U.S. or reduced ones by other countries, or a million and one other changes of the kind that are always occurring.

There are four, and only four ways, in which a country can adjust to such a disturbance and some combination of these ways must be used.

1. U.S. reserves of foreign currencies can be drawn down or foreign reserves of U.S. currency built up. In practice, this means that the U.S. government can let its stock of gold go down, since gold is exchangeable for foreign currencies, or it can borrow foreign currencies and make them available for dollars at official exchange rates; or foreign governments can accumulate dollars by selling U.S. residents foreign currencies at official rates. Reliance on reserves is obviously at best a temporary expedient. Indeed, it is precisely the extensive use by the U.S. of this expedient that accounts for the great concern with the balance of payments.

2. Domestic prices within the U.S. can be forced down relative to foreign prices. This is the main adjustment mechanism under a full-fledged gold standard. An initial deficit would produce an outflow of gold (mechanism 1, above); the outflow of gold would produce a decline in the stock of money; the decline in the stock of money would produce a fall in prices and incomes at home. At the same time, the reverse effects would occur abroad: the inflow of gold would expand the stock of money and thereby raise prices and income. Lowered U.S. prices and increased foreign prices would make U.S. goods more attractive to foreigners and thereby raise the number of dollars they wanted to buy; at the same time, the price changes would make foreign goods less attractive to U.S. residents and thereby lower the number of dollars they wanted to sell. Both effects would operate to reduce the deficit and restore balance without the necessity for further gold flows.

Under the modern managed standard, these effects are not automatic. Gold flows may still occur as the first step, but they will not affect the stock of money in either the country that loses, or the country that gains gold, unless the monetary authorities in the separate countries decide that they should. In every country today, the central bank or the Treasury has the power to offset the influence of gold flows, or to change the

stock of money without gold flows. Hence this mechanism
will be used only if the authorities in the country experiencing
the deficit are willing to produce a deflation, thereby creating
unemployment, in order to resolve its payments problem, or
the authorities in the country experiencing the surplus are
willing to produce an inflation.

3. Exactly the same effects can be achieved by a change in
exchange rates as by a change in domestic prices. For example,
suppose that under mechanism 2 the price of a particular car
in the United States fell by 10 per cent from $2,800 to $2,520.
If the price of the pound is throughout $2.80, this means that
the price in Britain (neglecting freight and other charges)
would fall from £1,000 to £900. Exactly the same decline in the
British price will occur without any change in the United
States price if the price of a pound rises from $2.80 to $3.11.
Formerly, the Englishman had to spend £1,000 to get $2,800.
Now he can get $2,800 for only £900. He would not know the
difference between this reduction in cost and the corresponding
reduction through a fall in the U.S. price without a change in
exchange rate.

In practice, there are several ways in which the change in
exchange rates can occur. With the kinds of pegged exchange
rates many countries now have, it can occur through devalua-
tion or appreciation, which is to say, a governmental declaration that it is changing the price at which it proposes to peg
its currency. Alternatively, the exchange rate does not need to be
pegged at all. It can be a market rate changing from day to
day, as was the case with the Canadian dollar from 1950 to
1962. If a market rate, it can be a truly free market rate determined primarily by private transactions as the Canadian rate
apparently was from 1952 to 1961, or it can be manipulated by
government speculation as was the situation in Britain from
1931 to 1939, and in Canada from 1950 to 1952 and again
from 1961 to 1962.

Of these various techniques, only the freely floating exchange rate is fully automatic and free from governmental
control.

4. The adjustments produced by mechanisms 2 and 3 consist of changes in flows of commodities and services induced

by changes either in internal prices or exchange rates. Instead, direct governmental controls or interferences with trade could be used to reduce attempted U.S. expenditures of dollars and expand U.S. receipts. Tariffs could be raised to choke off imports, subsidies could be given to stimulate exports, import quotas could be imposed on a variety of goods, capital investment abroad by U.S. citizens or firms could be controlled, and so on and on up to the whole paraphernalia of exchange controls. In this category must be included not only controls over private activities but also changes in governmental programs for balance of payments purposes. Recipients of foreign aid may be required to spend the aid in the U.S.; the military may procure goods in the United States at greater expense instead of abroad in order to save "dollars" — in the self-contradictory terminology used — and so on in bewildering array.

The important thing to note is that one or another of these four ways will and must be used. Double entry books must balance. Payments must equal receipts. The only question is how.

Our announced national policy has been and continues to be that we shall do none of these things. In a speech in December 1961, to the National Association of Manufacturers, President Kennedy stated "This administration, therefore, during its term of office — and I repeat this and make it as a flat statement — has no intention of imposing exchange controls, devaluing the dollar, raising trade barriers or choking off our economic recovery." As a matter of logic, this leaves only two possibilities: getting other countries to take the relevant measures, which is hardly a recourse that we can be sure of, or drawing down reserves, which the President and other officials repeatedly stated must not be permitted to continue. Yet *Time* magazine reports that the President's "promise drew a burst of applause" from the assembled businessmen. So far as our announced policy is concerned, we are in the position of a man living beyond his income who insists that he cannot possibly earn more, or spend less, or borrow, or finance the excess out of his assets!

Because we have been unwilling to adopt any one coherent policy, we and our trading partners — who make the same ostrich-like pronouncements as we do — have perforce been led to resort to all four mechanisms. In the early postwar years, U.S. reserves rose; more recently they have been declining. We welcomed inflation more readily than we otherwise would have when reserves were rising, and we have been more deflationary since 1958 than we would otherwise have been because of the drain of gold. Though we have not changed our official price of gold, our trading partners have changed theirs, and thereby the exchange rate between their currency and the dollar, and U.S. pressure has not been absent in producing these adjustments. Finally, our trading partners used direct controls extensively and, since we instead of they have been faced with deficits, we too have resorted to a wide range of direct interferences with payments, from reducing the amount of foreign goods that tourists can bring in free of duty — a trivial yet highly symptomatic step — to requiring foreign aid expenditures to be spent in the U.S., to keeping families from joining servicemen overseas, to more stringent import quotas on oil. We have been led also to engage in the demeaning step of asking foreign governments to take special measures to strengthen the U.S. balance of payments.

Of the four mechanisms, the use of direct controls is clearly the worst from almost any point of view and certainly the most destructive of a free society. Yet in lieu of any clear policy, we have been led increasingly to rely on such controls in one form or another. We preach publicly the virtues of free trade; yet we have been forced by the inexorable pressure of the balance of payments to move in the opposite direction and there is great danger that we shall move still farther. We can pass all the laws imaginable to reduce tariffs; the Administration may negotiate any number of tariff reductions; yet unless we adopt an alternative mechanism for resolving balance of payments deficits, we shall be led to substitute one set of trade impediments for another — indeed, to substitute a worse set for a better. While tariffs are bad, quotas and other direct interferences are even worse. A tariff, like a market price, is impersonal and does not involve direct interference by government in business affairs; a quota is likely to involve allocation and other administrative interferences, besides giving administrators valuable plums to pass out to private interests. Perhaps worse than either tariffs or quotas are extra-legal arrangements, such as the "voluntary" agreement by Japan to restrict textile exports.

FLOATING EXCHANGE RATES AS THE FREE MARKET SOLUTION

There are only two mechanisms that are consistent with a free market and free trade. One is a fully automatic international gold standard. This, as we saw in the preceding chapter, is neither feasible nor desirable. In any event, we cannot adopt it by ourselves. The other is a system of freely floating exchange rates determined in the market by private transactions without governmental intervention. This is the proper free-market counterpart to the monetary rule advocated in the preceding chapter. If we do not adopt it, we shall inevitably fail to expand the area of free trade and shall sooner or later be induced to impose widespread direct controls over trade. In this area, as in others, conditions can and do change unexpectedly. It may well be that we shall muddle through the difficulties that are facing us as this is written (April, 1962) and indeed that we may find ourselves in a surplus rather than deficit position, accumulating reserves rather than losing them. If so, this will only mean that other countries will be faced with the necessity of imposing controls. When, in 1950, I wrote an article proposing a system of floating exchange rates, it was in the context of European payments difficulties accompanying the then alleged "dollar shortage." Such a turnabout is always possible. Indeed, it is the very difficulty of predicting when and how such changes occur that is the basic argument for a free market. Our problem is not to "solve" *a* balance of payments problem. It is to solve *the* balance of payments problem by adopting a mechanism that will enable free market forces to provide a prompt, effective, and automatic response to changes in conditions affecting international trade.

Though freely floating exchange rates seem so clearly to be the appropriate free-market mechanism, they are strongly supported only by a fairly small number of liberals, mostly professional economists, and are opposed by many liberals who reject governmental intervention and governmental price-fixing in almost every other area. Why is this so? One reason is simply the tyranny of the status quo. A second reason is the confusion between a real gold standard and a pseudo gold standard. Under a real gold standard, the prices of different national currencies in terms of one another would be very nearly rigid since the different currencies would simply be different names for different amounts of gold. It is easy to make the mistake of supposing that we can get the substance of the real gold standard by the mere adoption of the form of a nominal obeisance to gold — the adoption of a pseudo gold standard under which the prices of different national currencies in terms of one another are rigid only because they are pegged prices in rigged markets. A third reason is the inevitable tendency for everyone to be in favor of a free market for everyone else, while regarding himself as deserving of special treatment. This particularly affects bankers in respect of exchange rates. They like to have a guaranteed price. Moreover, they are not familiar with the market devices that would arise to cope with fluctuations in exchange rates. The firms that would specialize in speculation and arbitrage in a free market for exchange do not exist. This is one way the tyranny of the status quo is enforced. In Canada, for example, some bankers, after a decade of a free rate which gave them a different status quo, were in the forefront of those favoring its continuation and objecting to either a pegged rate or government manipulation of the rate.

More important than any of these reasons, I believe, is a mistaken interpretation of experience with floating rates, arising out of a statistical fallacy that can be seen easily in a standard example. Arizona is clearly the worst place in the U.S. for a person with tuberculosis to go because the death rate from tuberculosis is higher in Arizona than in any other state. The fallacy is in this case obvious. It is less obvious in connection with exchange rates. When countries have gotten into severe financial difficulties through internal monetary mismanagement or for any other reason, they have had ultimately to resort to flexible exchange rates. No amount of exchange control or direct restrictions on trade enabled them to peg an exchange rate that was far out of line with economic realities. In consequence, it is unquestionably true that floating exchange rates have frequently been associated with financial and economic instability — as, for example, in hyperinflations, or severe but not hyperinflations such as have occurred in many South American countries. It is easy to conclude, as many have, that floating exchange rates produce such instability.

Being in favor of floating exchange rates does not mean being in favor of unstable exchange rates. When we support a free price system at home, this does not imply that we favor a system in which prices fluctuate wildly up and down. What we want is a system in which prices are free to fluctuate but in which the forces determining them are sufficiently stable so that in fact prices move within moderate ranges. This is equally true of a system of floating exchange rates. The ultimate objective is a world in which exchange rates, while free to vary, are, in fact, highly stable because basic economic policies and conditions are stable. Instability of exchange rates is a symptom of instability in the underlying economic structure. Elimination of this symptom by administrative freezing of exchange rates cures none of the underlying difficulties and only makes adjustments to them more painful.

THE POLICY MEASURES NECESSARY FOR A
FREE MARKET IN GOLD AND FOREIGN EXCHANGE

It may help bring out in concrete terms the implications of this discussion if I specify in detail the measures that I believe the U.S. should take to promote a truly free market in both gold and foreign exchange.

1. The U.S. should announce that it no longer commits itself to buy or sell gold at any fixed price.

2. Present laws making it illegal for individuals to own gold or to buy and sell gold should be repealed, so that there are no restrictions on the price at which gold can be bought or sold in terms of any other commodity or financial instrument, including national currencies.

3. The present law specifying that the Reserve System must hold gold certificates equal to 25 per cent of its liabilities should be repealed.

4. A major problem in getting rid completely of the gold price-support program, as of the wheat price-support program, is the transitional one of what to do with accumulated government stocks. In both cases, my own view is that the government should immediately restore a free market by instituting steps 1 and 2, and should ultimately dispose of all of its stocks. However, it would probably be desirable for the government to dispose of its stocks only gradually. For wheat, five years has always seemed to me a long enough period, so I have favored the government committing itself to dispose of one-fifth of its stocks in each of five years. This period seems reasonably satisfactory for gold as well. Hence, I propose that the government auction off its gold stocks on the free market over a five-year period. With a free gold market, individuals may well find warehouse certificates for gold more useful than actual gold. But if so, private enterprise can certainly provide the service of storing the gold and issuing certificates. Why should gold storage and the issuance of warehouse certificates be a nationalized industry?

5. The U.S. should announce also that it will not proclaim any official exchange rates between the dollar and other currencies and in addition that it will not engage in any speculative or other activities aimed at influencing exchange rates. These would then be determined in free markets.

6. These measures would conflict with our formal obligation as a member of the International Monetary Fund to specify an official parity for the dollar. However, the Fund found it possible to reconcile Canada's failure to specify a parity with its Articles and to give its approval to a floating rate for Canada. There is no reason why it cannot do the same for the U.S.

7. Other nations might choose to peg their currencies to the dollar. That is their business and there is no reason for us to object so long as we undertake no obligations to buy or sell their currency at a fixed price. They will be able to succeed in pegging their currency to ours only by one or more of the measures listed earlier — drawing on or accumulating reserves, co-ordinating their internal policy with U.S. policy, tightening or loosening direct controls on trade.

ELIMINATING U.S. RESTRICTIONS ON TRADE

A system such as that just outlined would solve the balance of payments problem once and for all. No deficit could possibly arise to require high government officials to plead with foreign countries and central banks for assistance, or to require an American President to behave like a harried country banker trying to restore confidence in his bank, or to force an administration preaching free trade to impose import restrictions, or to sacrifice important national and personal interests to the trivial question of the name of the currency in which payments are made. Payments would always balance because a price — the foreign exchange rate — would be free to produce a balance. No one could sell dollars unless he could find someone to buy them and conversely.

A system of floating exchange rates would therefore enable us to proceed effectively and directly toward complete free trade in goods and services — barring only such deliberate interference as may be justified on strictly political and military grounds; for example, banning the sale of strategic goods to communist countries. So long as we are firmly committed to the strait jacket of fixed exchange rates, we cannot move definitively to free trade. The possibility of tariffs or direct controls must be retained as an escape valve in case of necessity.

A system of floating exchange rates has the side advantage that it makes almost transparently obvious the fallacy in the most popular argument against free trade, the argument that "low" wages elsewhere make tariffs somehow necessary to protect "high" wages here. Is 100 yen an hour to a Japanese worker high or low compared with $4 an hour to an American worker? That all depends on the exchange rate. What determines the exchange rate? The necessity of making payments balance; i.e., of making the amount we can sell to the Japanese roughly equal to the amount they can sell to us.

Suppose for simplicity that Japan and the U.S. are the only two countries involved in trade and that at some exchange rate, say 1,000 yen to the dollar, Japanese could produce every single item capable of entering into foreign trade more cheaply than the U.S. At that exchange rate the Japanese could sell much to us, we, nothing to them. Suppose we pay them in paper dollars. What would the Japanese exporters do with the dollars? They cannot eat them, wear them, or live in them. If they were willing simply to hold them, then the printing industry—printing the dollar bills—would be a magnificent export industry. Its output would enable us all to have the good things of life provided nearly free by the Japanese.

But, of course, Japanese exporters would not want to hold the dollars. They would want to sell them for yen. By assumption, there is nothing they can buy for a dollar that they cannot buy for less than the 1,000 yen that a dollar will by assumption exchange for. This is equally true for other Japanese. Why then would any holder of yen give up 1,000 yen for a dollar that will buy less in goods than the 1,000 yen will? No one would. In order for the Japanese exporter to exchange his dollars for yen, he would have to offer to take fewer yen—the price of the dollar in terms of the yen would have to be less than 1,000, or of the yen in terms of the dollar more than 1 mill. But at 500 yen to the dollar Japanese goods are twice as expensive to Americans as before; American goods half as expensive to the Japanese. The Japanese will no longer be able to undersell American producers on all items.

Where will the price of the yen in terms of dollars settle? At whatever level is necessary to assure that all exporters who desire to do so can sell the dollars they get for the goods they export to America to importers who use them to buy goods in America. To speak loosely, at whatever level is necessary to assure that the value of U.S. exports (in dollars) is equal to the value of U.S. imports (again in dollars). Loosely, because a precise statement would have to take into account capital transactions, gifts, and so on. But these do not alter the central principle.

It will be noted that this discussion says nothing about the level of living of the Japanese worker or the American worker. These are irrelevant. If the Japanese worker has a lower standard of living than the American, it is because he is less productive on the average than the American, given the training he has, the amount of capital and land and so on that he has to work with. If the American worker is, let us say, on the average four times as productive as the Japanese worker, it is wasteful to use him to produce any goods in the production of which he is less than four times as productive. It is better to produce those goods at which he is more productive and trade them for the goods at which he is less productive. Tariffs do not assist the Japanese worker to raise his standard of living or protect the high standard of the American worker. On the contrary, they lower the Japanese standard and keep the American standard from being as high as it could be.

Given that we should move to free trade, how should we do so? The method that we have tried to adopt is reciprocal negotiation of tariff reductions with other countries. This seems to me a wrong procedure. In the first place, it ensures a slow pace. He moves fastest who moves alone. In the second place, it fosters an erroneous view of the basic problem. It makes it appear as if tariffs help the country imposing them but hurt other countries, as if when we reduce a tariff we give up something good and should get something in return in the form of a reduction in the tariffs imposed by other countries. In truth, the situation is quite different. Our tariffs hurt us as well as other countries. We would be benefited by dispensing with our tariffs even if other countries did not.[2] We would of course be benefited even more if they reduced theirs but our benefiting does not require that they reduce theirs. Self interests coincide and do not conflict.

I believe that it would be far better for us to move to free trade unilaterally, as Britain did in the nineteenth century when it repealed the corn laws. We, as they did, would experience an enormous accession of political and economic power. We are a great nation and it ill behooves us to require reciprocal benefits from Luxembourg before we reduce a tariff on Luxembourg products, or to throw thousands of Chinese refugees suddenly out of work by imposing import quotas on textiles from Hong Kong. Let us live up to our destiny and set the pace not be reluctant followers.

I have spoken in terms of tariffs for simplicity but, as already noted, non-tariff restrictions may now be more serious

[2] There are conceivable exceptions to these statements but, so far as I can see, they are theoretical curiosities, not relevant practical possibilities.

impediments to trade than tariffs. We should remove both. A prompt yet gradual program would be to legislate that all import quotas or other quantitative restrictions, whether imposed by us or "voluntarily" accepted by other countries, be raised 20 per cent a year until they are so high that they become irrelevant and can be abandoned, and that all tariffs be reduced by one-tenth of the present level in each of the next ten years.

There are few measures we could take that would do more to promote the cause of freedom at home and abroad. Instead of making grants to foreign governments in the name of economic aid — and thereby promoting socialism — while at the same time imposing restrictions on the products they succeed in producing — and thereby hindering free enterprise — we could assume a consistent and principled stance. We could say to the rest of the world: We believe in freedom and intend to practice it. No one can force you to be free. That is your business. But we can offer you full co-operation on equal terms to all. Our market is open to you. Sell here what you can and wish to. Use the proceeds to buy what you wish. In this way co-operation among individuals can be world wide yet free.

Chapter V

✦

Fiscal Policy

Ever since the new deal, a primary excuse for the expansion of governmental activity at the federal level has been the supposed necessity for government spending to eliminate unemployment. The excuse has gone through several stages. At first, government spending was needed to "prime the pump." Temporary expenditures would set the economy going and the government could then step out of the picture.

When the initial expenditures failed to eliminate unemployment and were followed by a sharp economic contraction in 1937–38, the theory of "secular stagnation" developed to justify a permanently high level of government spending. The economy had become mature, it was argued. Opportunities for investment had been largely exploited and no substantial new opportunities were likely to arise. Yet individuals would still want to save. Hence, it was essential for government to spend and run a perpetual deficit. The securities issued to finance the deficit would provide individuals with a way to accumulate savings while the government expenditures provided employment. This view has been thoroughly discredited by theoretical analysis and even more by actual experience, including the emergence of wholly new lines for private investment not dreamed of by the secular stagnationists. Yet it has left its heritage. The idea may be accepted by none, but the government programs undertaken in its name, like some of those intended to prime the pump, are still with us and indeed account for ever-growing government expenditures.

More recently, the emphasis has been on government expenditures neither to prime the pump nor to hold in check the specter of secular stagnation but as a balance wheel. When private expenditures decline for any reason, it is said, governmental expenditures should rise to keep total expenditures stable; conversely, when private expenditures rise, governmental expenditures should decline. Unfortunately, the balance wheel is unbalanced. Each recession, however minor, sends a shudder through politically sensitive legislators and administrators with their ever present fear that perhaps it is the harbinger of another 1929-33. They hasten to enact federal spending programs of one kind or another. Many of the programs do not in fact come into effect until after the recession has passed. Hence, insofar as they do affect total expenditures, on which I shall have more to say later, they tend to exacerbate the succeeding expansion rather than to mitigate the recession. The haste with which spending programs are approved is not matched by an equal haste to repeal them or to eliminate others when the recession is passed and expansion is under way. On the contrary, it is then argued that a "healthy" expansion must not be "jeopardized" by cuts in governmental expenditures. The chief harm done by the balance-wheel theory is therefore not that it has failed to offset recessions, which it has, and not that it has introduced an inflationary bias into governmental policy, which it has done too, but that it has continuously fostered an expansion in the range of governmental activities at the federal level and prevented a reduction in the burden of federal taxes.

In view of the emphasis on using the federal budget as a balance wheel, it is ironic that the most unstable component of national income in the postwar period is federal expenditure, and the instability has not at all been in a direction to offset movements of other expenditure components. Far from being a balance wheel offsetting other forces making for fluctuations, the federal budget has if anything been itself a major source of disturbance and instability.

Because its expenditures are now so large a part of the total for the economy as a whole, the federal government cannot avoid having significant effects on the economy. The first requisite is therefore that the government mend its own fences, that it adopt procedures that will lead to reasonable stability in its own flow of expenditures. If it would do that, it would make a clear contribution to reducing the adjustments required in the rest of the economy. Until it does that, it is farcical for government officials to adopt the self-righteous tones of the schoolmaster keeping unruly pupils in line. Of course, their doing so is not surprising. Passing the buck and blaming others for one's own deficiencies are not vices of which governmental officials have a monopoly.

Even if one were to accept the view that the federal budget should be and can be used as a balance wheel — a view I shall consider in more detail below — there is no necessity to use the expenditure side of the budget for this purpose. The tax side is equally available. A decline in national income automatically reduces the tax revenue of the federal government in greater proportion and thus shifts the budget in the direction of a deficit, and conversely during a boom. If it is desired to do more, taxes can be lowered during recessions and raised during expansions. Of course, politics might well enforce an asymmetry here too, making the declines politically more palatable than the rises.

If the balance-wheel theory has in practice been applied on the expenditure side, it has been because of the existence of other forces making for increased governmental expenditures; in particular, the widespread acceptance by intellectuals of the belief that government should play a larger role in economic and private affairs; the triumph, that is, of the philosophy of the welfare state. This philosophy has found a useful ally in the balance-wheel theory; it has enabled governmental intervention to proceed at a faster pace than would otherwise have been possible.

How different matters might now be if the balance-wheel theory had been applied on the tax side instead of the expenditure side. Suppose each recession had seen a cut in taxes and suppose the political unpopularity of raising taxes in the succeeding expansion had led to resistance to newly proposed governmental expenditure programs and to curtailment of existing ones. We might now be in a position where federal expenditures would be absorbing a good deal less of a national income that would be larger because of the reduction in the depressing and inhibiting effects of taxes.

I hasten to add that this dream is not intended to indicate support for the balance-wheel theory. In practice, even if the effects would be in the direction expected under the balance-wheel theory, they would be delayed in time and spread. To make them an effective offset to other forces making for fluctuations, we would have to be able to forecast those fluctuations a long time in advance. In fiscal policy as in monetary policy, all political considerations aside, we simply do not know enough to be able to use deliberate changes in taxation or expenditures as a sensitive stabilizing mechanism. In the process of trying to do so, we almost surely make matters worse. We make matters worse not by being consistently perverse — that would be easily cured by simply doing the opposite of what seemed at first the thing to do. We make matters worse by introducing a largely random disturbance that is simply added to other disturbances. That is what we seem in fact to have done in the past — in addition, of course to the major mistakes that have been seriously perverse. What I have written elsewhere in respect of monetary policy is equally applicable to fiscal policy: "What we need is not a skillful monetary driver of the economic vehicle continuously turning the steering wheel to adjust to the unexpected irregularities of the route, but some means of keeping the monetary passenger who is in the back seat as ballast from occasionally leaning over and giving the steering wheel a jerk that threatens to send the car off the road." [1]

For fiscal policy, the appropriate counterpart to the monetary rule would be to plan expenditure programs entirely in terms of what the community wants to do through government rather than privately, and without any regard to problems of year-to-year economic stability; to plan tax rates so as to provide sufficient revenues to cover planned expenditures on the average of one year with another, again without regard to year-to-year changes in economic stability; and to avoid erratic changes in either governmental expenditures or taxes. Of course, some changes may be unavoidable. A sudden change in the international situation may dictate large increases in military expenditures or permit welcome decreases. Such changes account for some erratic shifts in federal expenditures in the postwar period. But they by no means account for all.

Before leaving the subject of fiscal policy, I should like to discuss the view, now so widely held, that an increase in governmental expenditures relative to tax-receipts is necessarily expansionary and a decrease contractionary. This view, which is at the heart of the belief that fiscal policy can serve as a balance wheel, is by now almost taken for granted by businessmen, professional economists, and laymen alike. Yet it cannot be demonstrated to be true by logical considerations alone, has never been documented by empirical evidence, and is in fact inconsistent with the revelant empirical evidence of which I know.

The belief has its origin in a crude Keynesian analysis. Suppose governmental expenditures are raised by $100 and taxes are kept unchanged. Then, goes the simple analysis, on the first round, the people who receive the extra hundred dollars will have that much more income. They will save some of it, say one-third, and spend the remaining two-thirds. But this means that on the second round, someone else receives an extra $66 2/3 of income. He in turn will save some and spend some, and so on and on in infinite sequence. If at every stage

[1] *A Program for Monetary Stability*, (New York: Fordham University Press, 1959), p. 23.

one-third is saved and two-thirds spent, then the extra $100 of government expenditures will ultimately, on this analysis, add $300 to income. This is the simple Keynesian multiplier analysis with a multiplier of three. Of course, if there is one injection, the effects will die off, the initial jump in income of $100 being succeeded by a gradual decline back to the earlier level. But if government expenditures are kept $100 higher per unit of time, say $100 a year higher, then, on this analysis, income will remain higher by $300 a year.

This simple analysis is extremely appealing. But the appeal is spurious and arises from neglecting other relevant effects of the change in question. When these are taken into account, the final result is much more dubious: it may be anything from no change in income at all, in which case private expenditures will go down by the $100 by which government expenditures go up, to the full increase specified. And even if money income increases, prices may rise, so real income will increase less or not at all. Let us examine some of the possible slips 'twixt cup and lip.

In the first place, nothing is said in the simple account about what the government spends the $100 on. Suppose, for example, it spends it on something that individuals were otherwise obtaining for themselves. They were, for example, spending $100 on paying fees to a park which paid the cost of attendants to keep it clean. Suppose the government now pays these costs and permits people to enter the park "free." The attendants still receive the same income, but the people who paid the fees have $100 available. The government spending does not, even in the initial stage, add $100 to anyone's income. What it does is to leave some people with $100 available to use for purposes other than the park, and presumably purposes they value less highly. They can be expected to spend less out of their total income for consumer goods than formerly, since they are receiving the park services free. How much less, it is not easy to say. Even if we accept, as in the simple analysis, that people save one-third of additional income, it does not follow that when they get one set of consumer goods "free," two-thirds of the released money will be spent on other consumer goods. One extreme possibility, of course, is that they will continue to buy the same collection of other consumer goods as they did before and add the released $100 to their savings. In this case even in the simple Keynesian analysis, the effect of the government expenditures is completely offset: government expenditures go up by $100, private down by $100. Or, to take another example, the $100 may be spent to build a road that a private enterprise would otherwise have built or the availability of which may make repairs to the company's trucks unnecessary. The firm then has funds released, but presumably will not spend them all on what are less attractive investments. In these cases, government expenditures simply divert private expenditures and only the net excess of government expenditures is even available at the outset for the multiplier to work on. From this point of view, it is paradoxical that the way to assure no diversion is to have the government spend the money for something utterly useless — this is the limited intellectual content to the "filling-holes" type of make-work. But of course this itself shows that there is something wrong with the analysis.

In the second place, nothing is said in the simple account about where the government gets the $100 to spend. So far as the analysis goes, the results are the same whether the government prints extra money or borrows from the public. But surely which it does will make a difference. To separate fiscal from monetary policy, let us suppose the government borrows the $100 so that the stock of money is the same as it would have been in the absence of the government expenditure. This is the proper assumption because the stock of money can be increased without extra government expenditure, if that is desired, simply by printing the money and buying outstanding government bonds with it. But we must now ask what the effect of borrowing is. To analyze this problem, let us assume that diversion does not occur, so in the first instance there is no direct offset to the $100 in the form of a compensating drop in private expenditures. Note that the government's borrowing to spend does not alter the amount of money in private hands. The government borrows $100 with its right hand from some individuals and hands the money with its left hand to those individuals to whom its expenditures go. Different people hold the money but the total amount of money held is unchanged.

The simple Keynesian analysis implicitly assumes that borrowing the money does not have any effects on other spending. There are two extreme circumstances under which this can occur. First, suppose people are utterly indifferent to whether they hold bonds or money, so that bonds to get the $100 can be sold without having to offer a higher return to the buyer than such bonds were yielding before. (Of course, $100 is so small an amount that it would in practice have a negligible effect on the required rate of return, but the issue is one of principle whose practical effect can be seen by letting the $100 stand for $100 million or $100 ten-million.) In Keynesian jargon, there is a "liquidity trap" so people buy the bonds with "idle money." If this is not the case, and clearly it cannot be indefinitely, then the government can sell the bonds only by offering a higher rate of return on it. A higher rate will then have to be paid also by other borrowers. This higher rate will in general discourage private spending on the part of would-be borrowers. Here comes the second extreme circumstance under which the simple Keynesian analysis will hold: if potential borrowers are so stubborn about spending that no rise in interest rates however steep will cut down their expenditures, or, in Keynesian jargon, if the marginal efficiency schedule of investment is perfectly inelastic with respect to the interest rate.

I know of no established economist, no matter how much of a Keynesian he may regard himself as being, who would regard either of these extreme assumptions as holding currently, or as being capable of holding over any considerable range of borrowing or rise in interest rates, or as having held except under rather special circumstances in the past. Yet many an economist, let alone non-economist, whether regarding himself as Keynesian or not, accepts as valid the belief that a rise in governmental expenditures relative to tax receipts, even when financed by borrowing, is *necessarily* expansionist, though as we have seen, this belief implicitly requires one of these extreme circumstances to hold.

If neither assumption holds, the rise in government expenditures will be offset by a decline in private expenditures on the part either of those who lend funds to the government, or of those who would otherwise have borrowed the funds. How much of the rise in expenditures will be offset? This depends on the holders of money. The extreme assumption, implicit in a rigid quantity theory of money, is that the amount of money people want to hold depends, on the average, only on their income and not on the rate of return that they can get on bonds and similar securities. In this case, since the total stock of money is the same before and after, the total money income will also have to be the same in order to make people just satisfied to hold that money stock. This means that interest rates will have to rise enough to choke off an amount of private spending exactly equal to the increased public expenditure. In this extreme case, there is no sense at all in which the government expenditures are expansionary. Not even money income goes up, let alone real income. All that happens is that government expenditures go up and private expenditures down.

I warn the reader that this is a highly simplified analysis. A full analysis would require a lengthy textbook. But even this simplified analysis is enough to demonstrate that any result is possible between a $300 rise in income and a zero rise. The more stubborn consumers are with respect to how much they will spend on consumption out of a given income, and the more stubborn purchasers of capital goods are with respect to how much they will spend on such goods regardless of cost, the nearer the result will be to the Keynesian extreme of a $300 rise. On the other side, the more stubborn money holders are with respect to the ratio they wish to maintain between their cash balances and their income, the closer the result will be to the rigid quantity theory extreme of no change in income. In which of these respects the public is more stubborn is an empirical question to be judged from the factual evidence, not something that can be determined by reason alone.

Before the Great Depression of the 1930's, the bulk of economists would unquestionably have concluded that the result would be nearer to no rise in income than to a $300 rise. Since then, the bulk of economists would unquestionably conclude the opposite. More recently, there has been a movement back toward the earlier position. Sad to say, none of these shifts can be said to be based on satisfactory evidence. They have been based rather on intuitive judgments from crude experience.

In co-operation with some of my students, I have done some fairly extensive empirical work, for the U.S. and other countries, to get some more satisfactory evidence.[2] The results are striking. They strongly suggest that the actual outcome will be closer to the quantity theory extreme than to the Keynesian. The judgement that seems justified on the basis of this evidence is that the assumed $100 increase in government expenditures can on the average be expected to add just about $100 to income, sometimes less, sometimes more. This means that a rise in government expenditures relative to income is not expansionary in any relevant sense. It may add to money income but all of this addition is absorbed by government expenditures. Private expenditures are unchanged. Since prices are likely to rise in the process, or fall less than they otherwise would, the effect is to leave private expenditures smaller in real terms. Converse propositions hold for a decline in government expenditures.

These conclusions cannot of course be regarded as final. They are based on the broadest and most comprehensive body of evidence I know about, but that body of evidence still leaves much to be desired.

One thing is however clear. Whether the views so widely accepted about the effects of fiscal policy be right or wrong, they are contradicted by at least one extensive body of evidence. I know of no other coherent or organized body of evidence justifying them. They are part of economic mythology, not the demonstrated conclusions of economic analysis or quantitative studies. Yet they have wielded immense influence in securing widespread public backing for far-reaching governmental interference in economic life.

[2] Some of the results are contained in Milton Friedman and David Meiselman, *The Relative Stability of the Investment Multiplier and Monetary Velocity in the United States, 1896–1958* (forthcoming publication of Commission on Money and Credit).

Chapter VI

The Role of Government
in Education

FORMAL SCHOOLING is today paid for and almost entirely administered by government bodies or non-profit institutions. This situation has developed gradually and is now taken so much for granted that little explicit attention is any longer directed to the reasons for the special treatment of schooling even in countries that are predominantly free enterprise in organization and philosophy. The result has been an indiscriminate extension of governmental responsibility.

In terms of the principles developed in chapter ii, governmental intervention into education can be rationalized on two grounds. The first is the existence of substantial "neighborhood effects," i.e., circumstances under which the action of one individual imposes significant costs on other individuals for which it is not feasible to make him compensate them, or yields significant gains to other individuals for which it is not feasible to make them compensate him — circumstances that make voluntary exchange impossible. The second is the paternalistic concern for children and other irresponsible individuals. Neighborhood effects and paternalism have very different implications for (1) general education for citizenship, and (2) specialized vocational education. The grounds for governmental intervention are widely different in these two areas and justify very different types of action.

One further preliminary remark: it is important to distinguish between "schooling" and "education." Not all schooling is education nor all education, schooling. The proper subject of concern is education. The activities of government are mostly limited to schooling.

GENERAL EDUCATION FOR CITIZENSHIP

A stable and democratic society is impossible without a minimum degree of literacy and knowledge on the part of most citizens and without widespread acceptance of some common set of values. Education can contribute to both. In consequence, the gain from the education of a child accrues not only to the child or to his parents but also to other members of the society. The education of my child contributes to your welfare by promoting a stable and democratic society. It is not feasible to identify the particular individuals (or families) benefited and so to charge for the services rendered. There is therefore a significant "neighborhood effect."

What kind of governmental action is justified by this particular neighborhood effect? The most obvious is to require that each child receive a minimum amount of schooling of a specified kind. Such a requirement could be imposed upon the parents without further government action, just as owners of buildings, and frequently of automobiles, are required to adhere to specified standards to protect the safety of others. There is, however, a difference between the two cases. Individuals who cannot pay the costs of meeting the standards required for buildings or automobiles can generally divest themselves of the property by selling it. The requirement can thus generally be enforced without government subsidy. The separation of a child from a parent who cannot pay for the minimum required schooling is clearly inconsistent with our reliance on the family as the basic social unit and our belief in the freedom of the individual. Moreover, it would be very likely to detract from his education for citizenship in a free society.

If the financial burden imposed by such a schooling requirement could readily be met by the great bulk of the families in a community, it might still be both feasible and desirable to require the parents to meet the cost directly. Extreme cases could be handled by special subsidy provisions for needy families. There are many areas in the United States today where these conditions are satisfied. In these areas, it would be highly desirable to impose the costs directly on the parents. This would eliminate the governmental machinery now required to collect tax funds from all residents during the whole of their lives and then pay it back mostly to the same people during the period when their children are in school. It would reduce the likelihood that governments would also administer schools, a matter discussed further below. It would increase the likelihood that the subsidy component of school expenditures would decline as the need for such subsidies declined with increasing general levels of income. If, as now, the government pays for all or most schooling, a rise in income simply leads to a still larger circular flow of funds through the tax mechanism, and an expansion in the role of the government. Finally, but by no means least, imposing the costs on the parents would tend to equalize the social and private costs of having children and so promote a better distribution of families by size.[1]

Differences among families in resources and in number of children, plus the imposition of a standard of schooling involving very sizable costs, make such a policy hardly feasible in many parts of the United States. Both in such areas, and in

---

[1] It is by no means so fantastic as may appear that such a step would noticeably affect the size of families. For example, one explanation of the lower birth rate among higher than among lower socio-economic groups may well be that children are relatively more expensive to the former, thanks in considerable measure to the higher standards of schooling they maintain, the costs of which they bear.

areas where such a policy would be feasible, government has instead assumed the financial costs of providing schooling. It has paid, not only for the minimum amount of schooling required of all, but also for additional schooling at higher levels available to youngsters but not required of them. One argument for both steps is the "neighborhood effects" discussed above. The costs are paid because this is the only feasible means of enforcing the required minimum. Additional schooling is financed because other people benefit from the schooling of those of greater ability and interest, since this is a way of providing better social and political leadership. The gain from these measures must be balanced against the costs, and there can be much honest difference of judgment about how extensive a subsidy is justified. Most of us, however, would probably conclude that the gains are sufficiently important to justify some government subsidy.

These grounds justify government subsidy of only certain kinds of schooling. To anticipate, they do not justify subsidizing purely vocational training which increases the economic productivity of the student but does not train him for either citizenship or leadership. It is extremely difficult to draw a sharp line between the two types of schooling. Most general schooling adds to the economic value of the student—indeed it is only in modern times and in a few countries that literacy has ceased to have a marketable value. And much vocational training broadens the student's outlook. Yet the distinction is meaningful. Subsidizing the training of veterinarians, beauticians, dentists, and a host of other specialists, as is widely done in the United States in governmentally supported educational institutions, cannot be justified on the same grounds as subsidizing elementary schools or, at a higher level, liberal arts colleges. Whether it can be justified on quite different grounds will be discussed later in this chapter.

The qualitative argument from "neighborhood effects" does not, of course, determine the specific kinds of schooling that should be subsidized or by how much they should be subsidized. The social gain presumably is greatest for the lowest levels of schooling, where there is the nearest approach to unanimity about content, and declines continuously as the level of schooling rises. Even this statement cannot be taken completely for granted. Many governments subsidized universities long before they subsidized lower schools. What forms of education have the greatest social advantage and how much of the community's limited resources should be spent on them must be decided by the judgment of the community expressed through its accepted political channels. The aim of this analysis is not to decide these questions for the community but rather to clarify the issues involved in making a choice, in particular whether it is appropriate to make the choice on a communal rather than individual basis.

As we have seen, both the imposition of a minimum required level of schooling and the financing of this schooling by the state can be justified by the "neighborhood effects" of schooling. A third step, namely the actual administration of educational institutions by the government, the "nationalization," as it were, of the bulk of the "education industry" is much more difficult to justify on these, or, so far as I can see, any other, grounds. The desirability of such nationalization has seldom been faced explicitly. Governments have, in the main, financed schooling by paying directly the costs of running educational institutions. Thus this step seemed required by the decision to subsidize schooling. Yet the two steps could readily be separated. Governments could require a minimum level of schooling financed by giving parents vouchers redeemable for a specified maximum sum per child per year if spent on "approved" educational services. Parents would then be free to spend this sum and any additional sum they themselves provided on purchasing educational services from an "approved" institution of their own choice. The educational services could be rendered by private enterprises operated for profit, or by non-profit institutions. The role of the government would be limited to insuring that the schools met certain minimum standards, such as the inclusion of a minimum common content in their programs, much as it now inspects restaurants to insure that they maintain minimum sanitary standards. An excellent example of a program of this sort is the United States educational program for veterans after World War II. Each veteran who qualified was given a maximum sum per year that could be spent at any institution of his choice, provided it met certain minimum standards. A more limited example is the provision in Britain whereby local authorities pay the fees of some students attending non-state schools. Another is the arrangement in France whereby the state pays part of the costs for students attending non-state schools.

One argument for nationalizing schools resting on a "neighborhood effect" is that it might otherwise be impossible to provide the common core of values deemed requisite for social stability. The imposition of minimum standards on privately conducted schools, as suggested above, might not be enough to achieve this result. The issue can be illustrated concretely in terms of schools run by different religious groups. Such schools, it can be argued, will instil sets of values that are inconsistent with one another and with those instilled in nonsectarian schools; in this way, they convert education into a divisive rather than a unifying force.

Carried to its extreme, this argument would call not only for governmentally administered schools, but also for compulsory attendance at such schools. Existing arrangements in the United States and most other Western countries are a halfway house. Governmentally administered schools are available but not compulsory. However, the link between the financing of schooling and its administration places other schools at a disadvantage: they get the benefit of little or none of the governmental funds spent on schooling — a situation that has been the source of much political dispute, particularly in France and at present in the United States. The elimination of this disadvantage might, it is feared, greatly strengthen the parochial schools and so render the problem of achieving a common core of values even more difficult.

Persuasive as this argument is, it is by no means clear that it is valid or that denationalizing schooling would have the effects suggested. On grounds of principle, it conflicts with the preservation of freedom itself. Drawing a line between providing for the common social values required for a stable society, on the one hand, and indoctrination inhibiting freedom of thought and belief, on the other is another of those vague boundaries that is easier to mention than to define.

In terms of effects, denationalizing schooling would widen the range of choice available to parents. If, as at present, parents can send their children to public schools without special payment, very few can or will send them to other schools unless they too are subsidized. Parochial schools are at a disadvantage in not getting any of the public funds devoted to schooling, but they have the compensating advantage of being run by institutions that are willing to subsidize them and can raise funds to do so. There are few other sources of subsidies for private schools. If present public expenditures on schooling were made available to parents regardless of where they send their children, a wide variety of schools would spring up to meet the demand. Parents could express their views about schools directly by withdrawing their children from one school and sending them to another, to a much greater extent than is now possible. In general, they can now take this step only at considerable cost — by sending their children to a private school or by changing their residence. For the rest, they can express their views only through cumbrous political channels. Perhaps a somewhat greater degree of freedom to choose schools could be made available in a governmentally administered system, but it would be difficult to carry this freedom very far in view of the obligation to provide every child with a place. Here, as in other fields, competitive enterprise is likely to be far more efficient in meeting consumer demand than either nationalized enterprises or enterprises run to serve other purposes. The final result may therefore be that parochial schools would decline rather than grow in importance.

A related factor working in the same direction is the understandable reluctance of parents who send their children to parochial schools to increase taxes to finance higher public school expenditures. As a result, those areas where parochial schools are important have great difficulty raising funds for public schools. Insofar as quality is related to expenditure, as to some extent it undoubtedly is, public schools tend to be of lower quality in such areas and hence parochial schools are relatively more attractive.

Another special case of the argument that governmentally conducted schools are necessary for education to be a unifying force is that private schools would tend to exacerbate class distinctions. Given greater freedom about where to send their children, parents of a kind would flock together and so prevent a healthy intermingling of children from decidedly different backgrounds. Whether or not this argument is valid in principle, it is not at all clear that the stated results would follow. Under present arrangements, stratification of residential areas effectively restricts the intermingling of children from decidedly different backgrounds. In addition, parents are not now prevented from sending their children to private schools. Only a highly limited class can or does do so, parochial schools aside, thus producing further stratification.

Indeed, this argument seems to me to point in almost the diametrically opposite direction — toward the denationalizing of schools. Ask yourself in what respect the inhabitant of a low income neighborhood, let alone of a Negro neighborhood in a large city, is most disadvantaged. If he attaches enough importance to, say, a new automobile, he can, by dint of saving, accumulate enough money to buy the same car as a resident of a high-income suburb. To do so, he need not move to that suburb. On the contrary, he can get the money partly by economizing on his living quarters. And this goes equally for clothes, or furniture, or books, or what not. But let a poor family in a slum have a gifted child and let it set such high value on his or her schooling that it is willing to scrimp and save for the purpose. Unless it can get special treatment, or scholarship assistance, at one of the very few private schools, the family is in a very difficult position. The "good" public schools are in the high income neighborhoods. The family might be willing to spend something in addition to what it pays in taxes to get better schooling for its child. But it can hardly afford simultaneously to move to the expensive neighborhood.

Our views in these respects are, I believe, still dominated by the small town which had but one school for the poor and rich residents alike. Under such circumstances, public schools may well have equalized opportunities. With the growth of urban and suburban areas, the situation has changed drastically. Our present school system, far from equalizing opportunity, very likely does the opposite. It makes it all the harder for the exceptional few — and it is they who are the hope of the future — to rise above the poverty of their initial state.

Another argument for nationalizing schooling is "technical monopoly." In small communities and rural areas, the number of children may be too small to justify more than one school of reasonable size, so that competition cannot be relied on to protect the interests of parents and children. As in other cases of technical monopoly, the alternatives are unrestricted private monopoly, state-controlled private monopoly, and public operation — a choice among evils. This argument, though clearly valid and significant, has been greatly weakened in recent decades by improvements in transportation and increasing concentration of the population in urban communities.

The arrangement that perhaps comes closest to being justified by these considerations — at least for primary and secondary education — is a combination of public and private schools. Parents who choose to send their children to private schools would be paid a sum equal to the estimated cost of educating a child in a public school, provided that at least this sum was spent on education in an approved school. This arrangement would meet the valid features of the "technical monopoly" argument. It would meet the just complaints of parents that if they send their children to private non-subsidized schools they are required to pay twice for education — once in the form of general taxes and once directly. It would permit competition to develop. The development and improvement of all schools would thus be stimulated. The injection of competition would do much to promote a healthy variety of schools. It would do much, also, to introduce flexibility into school systems. Not least of its benefits would be to make the salaries of school teachers responsive to market forces. It would thereby give public authorities an independent standard against which to judge salary scales and promote a more rapid adjustment to changes in conditions of demand and supply.

It is widely urged that the great need in schooling is more money to build more facilities and to pay higher salaries to teachers in order to attract better teachers. This seems a false diagnosis. The amount of money spent on schooling has been rising at an extraordinarily high rate, far faster than our total income. Teachers' salaries have been rising far faster than returns in comparable occupations. The problem is not primarily that we are spending too little money — though we may be — but that we are getting so little per dollar spent. Perhaps the amounts of money spent on magnificent structures and luxurious grounds at many schools are properly classified as expenditures on schooling. It is hard to accept them equally as expenditures on education. And this is equally clear with respect to courses in basket weaving, social dancing, and the numerous other special subjects that do such credit to the ingenuity of educators. I hasten to add that there can be no conceivable objection to parents' spending their own money on such frills if they wish. That is their business. The objection is to using money raised by taxation imposed on parents and nonparents alike for such purposes. Wherein are the "neighborhood effects" that justify such use of tax money?

A major reason for this kind of use of public money is the present system of combining the administration of schools with their financing. The parent who would prefer to see money used for better teachers and texts rather than coaches and corridors has no way of expressing this preference except by persuading a majority to change the mixture for all. This is a special case of the general principle that a market permits each to satisfy his own taste — effective proportional representation; whereas the political process imposes conformity. In addition, the parent who would like to spend some extra money on his child's education is greatly limited. He cannot add something to the amount now being spent to school his child and transfer his child to a correspondingly more costly school. If he does transfer his child, he must pay the whole cost and not simply the additional cost. He can only spend extra money easily on extra-curricular activities — dancing lessons, music lessons, etc. Since the private outlets for spending more money on schooling are so blocked, the pressure to spend more on the education of children manifests itself in ever higher public expenditures on items ever more tenuously related to the basic justification for governmental intervention into schooling.

As this analysis implies, the adoption of the suggested arrangements might well mean smaller governmental expenditures on schooling, yet higher total expenditures. It would enable parents to buy what they want more efficiently and thereby lead them to spend more than they now do directly and indirectly through taxation. It would prevent parents from being frustrated in spending more money on schooling by both the present need for conformity in how the money is spent and by the understandable reluctance on the part of persons not currently having children in school, and especially those who will not in the future have them in school, to impose higher taxes on themselves for purposes often far removed from education as they understand the term.[2]

With respect to teachers' salaries, the major problem is not that they are too low on the average — they may well be too high on the average — but that they are too uniform and rigid. Poor teachers are grossly overpaid and good teachers grossly underpaid. Salary schedules tend to be uniform and determined far more by seniority, degrees received, and teaching certificates acquired than by merit. This, too, is largely a result of the present system of governmental administration of schools and becomes more serious as the unit over which governmental control is exercised becomes larger. Indeed, this very fact is a major reason why professional educational organizations so strongly favor broadening the unit — from the local school district to the state, from the state to the federal government. In any bureaucratic, essentially civil-service organization, standard salary scales are almost inevitable; it is next to impossible to simulate competition capable of providing wide differences in salaries according to merit. The educators, which means the teachers themselves, come to exercise primary control. The parent or local community comes to exercise little control. In any area, whether it be carpentry or plumbing or teaching, the majority of workers favor standard salary scales and oppose merit differentials, for the obvious reason that the

[2] A striking example of the same effect in another field is the British National Health Service. In a careful and penetrating study, D. S. Lees establishes rather conclusively that, "Far from being extravagant, expenditure on NHS has been less than consumers would probably have chosen to spend in a free market. The record of hospital building in particular has been deplorable." "Health Through Choice," *Hobart Paper 14* (London: Institute of Economic Affairs, 1961), p. 58.

specially talented are always few. This is a special case of the
general tendency for people to seek to collude to fix prices,
whether through unions or industrial monopolies. But collusive agreements will generally be destroyed by competition unless the government enforces them, or at least renders them
considerable support.

If one were to seek deliberately to devise a system of recruit-
ing and paying teachers calculated to repel the imaginative
and daring and self-confident and to attract the dull and medi-
ocre and uninspiring, he could hardly do better than imitate
the system of requiring teaching certificates and enforcing
standard salary structures that has developed in the larger
city and state-wide systems. It is perhaps surprising that the
level of ability in elementary and secondary school teaching is
as high as it is under these circumstances. The alternative system would resolve these problems and permit competition
to be effective in rewarding merit and attracting ability to
teaching.

Why has governmental intervention in schooling in the
United States developed along the lines it has? I do not have
the detailed knowledge of educational history that would be
required to answer this question definitively. A few conjec-
tures may nonetheless be useful to suggest the kinds of considerations that may alter the appropriate social policy. I am by
no means sure that the arrangements I now propose would in
fact have been desirable a century ago. Before the extensive
growth in transportation, the "technical monopoly" argument
was much stronger. Equally important, the major problem in
the United States in the nineteenth and early twentieth century was not to promote diversity but to create the core of
common values essential to a stable society. Great streams of
immigrants were flooding the United States from all over the
world, speaking different languages and observing diverse
customs. The "melting pot" had to introduce some measure of
conformity and loyalty to common values. The public school
had an important function in this task, not least by imposing
English as a common language. Under the alternative voucher
scheme, the minimum standards imposed on schools to qualify for approval could have included the use of English. But it

might well have been more difficult to insure that this requirement was imposed and satisfied in a private school system. I
do not mean to conclude that the public school system was
definitely preferable to the alternative, but only that a far
stronger case could have been made for it then than now. Our
problem today is not to enforce conformity; it is rather that we
are threatened with an excess of conformity. Our problem is
to foster diversity, and the alternative would do this far more
effectively than a nationalized school system.

Another factor that may have been important a century ago
was the combination of the general disrepute of cash grants to
individuals ("handouts"), with the absence of an efficient administrative machinery to handle the distribution of vouchers
and check their use. Such machinery is a phenomenon of modern times that has come to full flower with the enormous extension of personal taxation and of social security programs. In
its absence, the administration of schools may have been regarded as the only possible way to finance education.

As some of the examples cited above (England and France)
suggest, some features of the proposed arrangements are present in existing educational systems. And there has been strong
and, I believe, increasing pressure for arrangements of this
kind in most Western countries. This is perhaps partly explained by modern developments in governmental administrative machinery that facilitate such arrangements.

Although many administrative problems would arise in
changing over from the present to the proposed system and in
its administration, these seem neither insoluble nor unique. As
in the denationalization of other activities, existing premises
and equipment could be sold to private enterprises that wanted
to enter the field. Thus, there would be no waste of capital in
the transition. Since governmental units, at least in some areas,
would continue to administer schools, the transition would be
gradual and easy. The local administration of schooling in the
United States and some other countries would similarly facilitate the transition, since it would encourage experimentation
on a small scale. Difficulties would doubtless arise in determining eligibility for grants from a particular governmental unit,
but this is identical with the existing problem of determining

which unit is obligated to provide schooling facilities for a particular child. Differences in size of grants would make one
area more attractive than another just as differences in the
quality of schooling now have the same effect. The only additional complication is a possibly greater opportunity for abuse
because of the greater freedom to decide where to educate
children. Supposed difficulty of administration is a standard
defense of the status quo against any proposed change; in this
particular case, it is an even weaker defense than usual because existing arrangements must master not only the major
problems raised by the proposed arrangements but also the
additional problems raised by the administration of schools as
a governmental function.

SCHOOLING AT COLLEGE AND UNIVERSITY LEVEL

The preceding discussion is concerned mostly with primary
and secondary schooling. For higher schooling, the case for
nationalization on grounds either of neighborhood effects or
of technical monopoly is even weaker. For the lowest levels of
schooling, there is considerable agreement, approximating
unanimity, on the appropriate content of an educational program for citizens of a democracy — the three R's cover most of
the ground. At successively higher levels, there is less and less
agreement. Surely, well below the level of the American college, there is insufficient agreement to justify imposing the
views of a majority, much less a plurality, on all. The lack of
agreement may, indeed, extend so far as to cast doubts on the
appropriateness even of subsidizing schooling at this level; it
surely goes far enough to undermine any case for nationalization on the grounds of providing a common core of values.
There can hardly be any question of "technical monopoly" at
this level, in view of the distances that individuals can and do
go to attend institutions of higher learning.

Governmental institutions play a smaller role in the United
States in higher schooling than at primary and secondary
levels. Yet they grew greatly in importance, certainly until
the 1920's, and now account for more than half of the students

attending colleges and universities.[3] One of the main reasons for their growth was their relative cheapness; most state and municipal colleges and universities charge much lower tuition fees than private universities can afford to charge. Private universities have in consequence had serious financial problems, and have quite properly complained of "unfair" competition. They have wanted to maintain their independence from government, yet at the same time have felt driven by financial pressure to seek government aid.

The preceding analysis suggests the lines along which a satisfactory solution can be sought. Public expenditures on higher schooling can be justified as a means of training youngsters for citizenship and for community leadership — though I hasten to add that the large fraction of current expenditure that goes for strictly vocational training cannot be justified in this way, or indeed, as we shall see, in any other. Restricting the subsidy to schooling obtained at a state-administered institution cannot be justified on any grounds. Any subsidy should be granted to individuals to be spent at institutions of their own choosing, provided only that the schooling is of a kind that it is desired to subsidize. Any government schools that are retained should charge fees covering educational costs and so compete on an equal level with non-government-supported schools.[4] The resulting system would follow in its broad outlines the arrangements adopted in the United States after World War II for financing the education of veterans, except that the funds would presumably come from the states rather than the federal government.

The adoption of such arrangements would make for more effective competition among various types of schools and for a more efficient utilization of their resources. It would eliminate the pressure for direct government assistance to private colleges and universities and thus preserve their full independence and diversity at the same time as it enabled them to grow

[3] See George J. Stigler, *Employment and Compensation in Education* ("Occasional Paper" No. 33, [New York: National Bureau of Economic Research, 1950]), p. 33.

[4] I am abstracting from expenditures on basic research. I have interpreted schooling narrowly so as to exclude considerations that would open up an unduly wide field.

relative to state institutions. It might also have the ancillary advantage of causing scrutiny of the purposes for which subsidies are granted. The subsidization of institutions rather than of people has led to an indiscriminate subsidization of all activities appropriate for such institutions, rather than of the activities appropriate for the state to subsidize. Even cursory examination suggests that while the two classes of activities overlap, they are far from identical.

The equity argument for the alternative arrangement is particularly clear at college and university levels because of the existence of a large number and variety of private schools. The state of Ohio, for example, says to its citizens: "If you have a youngster who wants to go to college, we shall automatically grant him or her a sizable four-year scholarship, provided that he or she can satisfy rather minimal education requirements, and provided further that he or she is smart enough to choose to go to the University of Ohio. If your youngster wants to go, or you want him or her to go, to Oberlin College, or Western Reserve University, let alone to Yale, Harvard, Northwestern, Beloit, or the University of Chicago, not a penny for him." How can such a program be justified? Would it not be far more equitable, and promote a higher standard of scholarship, to devote such money as the state of Ohio wished to spend on higher education to scholarships tenable at any college or university and to require the University of Ohio to compete on equal terms with other colleges and universities? [5]

VOCATIONAL AND PROFESSIONAL SCHOOLING

Vocational and professional schooling has no neighborhood effects of the kind attributed above to general education. It is a form of investment in human capital precisely analogous to investment in machinery, buildings, or other forms of non-human capital. Its function is to raise the economic productiv-

[5] I have used Ohio rather than Illinois, because since the article of which this chapter is a revision was written (1953), Illinois has adopted a program going part-way along this line by providing scholarships tenable at private colleges and universities in Illinois. California has done the same. Virginia has adopted a similar program at lower levels for a very different reason, to avoid racial integration. The Virginia case is discussed in chapter vii.

ity of the human being. If it does so, the individual is rewarded in a free enterprise society by receiving a higher return for his services than he would otherwise be able to command.[6] This difference in return is the economic incentive to invest capital whether in the form of a machine or a human being. In both cases, extra returns must be balanced against the costs of acquiring them. For vocational schooling, the major costs are the income foregone during the period of training, interest lost by postponing the beginning of the earning period, and special expenses of acquiring the training such as tuition fees and expenditures on books and equipment. For physical capital, the major costs are the expense of constructing the capital equipment and the interest foregone during construction. In both cases, an individual presumably regards the investment as desirable if the extra returns, as he views them, exceed the extra costs, as he views them.[7] In both cases, if the individual undertakes the investment and if the state neither subsidizes the investment nor taxes the return, the individual (or his parents, sponsor, or benefactor) in general bears all the extra costs and receives all the extra returns: there are no obvious unborne costs or unappropriable returns that tend to make private incentives diverge systematically from those that are socially appropriate.

If capital were as readily available for investment in human beings as for investment in physical assets, whether through the market or through direct investment by the individuals concerned, or their parents or benefactors, the rate of return on capital would tend to be roughly equal in the two fields. If it were higher on non-human capital, parents would have an incentive to buy such capital for their children instead of investing a corresponding sum in vocational training, and conversely. In fact, however, there is considerable empirical evi-

[6] The increased return may be only partly in a monetary form; it may also consist of non-pecuniary advantages attached to the occupation for which the vocational training fits the individual. Similarly, the occupation may have non-pecuniary disadvantages, which would have to be reckoned among the costs of the investment.

[7] For a more detailed and precise statement of the considerations entering into the choice of an occupation, see Milton Friedman and Simon Kuznets, *Income from Independent Professional Practice* (New York: National Bureau of Economic Research, 1945), pp. 81–95, 118–37.

dence that the rate of return on investment in training is very much higher than the rate of return on investment in physical capital. This difference suggests the existence of underinvestment in human capital.[8]

This underinvestment in human capital presumably reflects an imperfection in the capital market. Investment in human beings cannot be financed on the same terms or with the same ease as investment in physical capital. It is easy to see why. If a fixed money loan is made to finance investment in physical capital, the lender can get some security for his loan in the form of a mortgage or residual claim to the physical asset itself, and he can count on realizing at least part of his investment in case of default by selling the physical asset. If he makes a comparable loan to increase the earning power of a human being, he clearly cannot get any comparable security. In a non-slave state, the individual embodying the investment cannot be bought and sold. Even if he could, the security would not be comparable. The productivity of the physical capital does not in general depend on the co-operativeness of the original borrower. The productivity of the human capital quite obviously does. A loan to finance the training of an individual who has no security to offer other than his future earnings is therefore a much less attractive proposition than a loan to finance the erection of a building: the security is less, and the cost of subsequent collection of interest and principal is very much greater.

A further complication is introduced by the inappropriateness of fixed money loans to finance investment in training. Such an investment necessarily involves much risk. The average expected return may be high, but there is wide variation about the average. Death or physical incapacity is one obvious source of variation but this is probably much less important than differences in ability, energy, and good fortune. Consequently if fixed money loans were made, and were secured only by expected future earnings, a considerable fraction would never be repaid. In order to make such loans attractive to lenders, the nominal interest rate charged on all loans would

[8] See G. S. Becker, "Underinvestment in College Education?" *American Economic Review, Proceedings* L (1960), 356–64; T. W. Schultz, "Investment in human Capital," *American Economic Review*, LXI (1961), 1–17.

have to be sufficiently high to compensate for the capital losses on the defaulted loans. The high nominal interest rate would both conflict with usury laws and make the loans unattractive to borrowers.[9] The device adopted to meet the corresponding problem for other risky investments is equity investment plus limited liability on the part of the shareholders. The counterpart for education would be to "buy" a share in an individual's earning prospects; to advance him the funds needed to finance his training on condition that he agree to pay the lender a specified fraction of his future earnings. In this way, a lender would get back more than his initial investment from relatively successful individuals, which would compensate for the failure to recoup his original investment from the unsuccessful.

There seems no legal obstacle to private contracts of this kind, even though they are economically equivalent to the purchase of a share in an individual's earning capacity and thus to partial slavery. One reason why such contracts have not become common, despite their potential profitability to both lender and borrower, is presumably the high costs of administering them, given the freedom of individuals to move from one place to another, the need for getting accurate income statements, and the long period over which the contracts would run. These costs would presumably be particularly high for investment on a small scale with a wide geographical spread of the individuals financed. Such costs may well be the primary reason that this type of investment has never developed under private auspices.

It seems highly likely, however, that a major role has also

[9] Despite these obstacles to fixed money loans, I am told that they have been a very common means of financing education in Sweden, where they have apparently been available at moderate rates of interest. Presumably a proximate explanation is a smaller dispersion of income among university graduates than in the United States. But this is no ultimate explanation and may not be the only or major reason for the difference in practice. Further study of Swedish and similar experience is highly desirable to test whether the reasons given above are adequate to explain the absence in the United States and other countries of a highly developed market in loans to finance vocational education, or whether there may not be other obstacles that could be removed more easily.

In recent years, there has been an encouraging development in the U.S. of private loans to college students. The main development has been stimulated by United Student Aid Funds, a non-profit institution which underwrites loans made by individual banks.

been played by the cumulative effect of the novelty of the idea, the reluctance to think of investment in human beings as strictly comparable to investment in physical assets, the resultant likelihood of irrational public condemnation of such contracts, even if voluntarily entered into, and legal and conventional limitations on the kind of investments that may be made by the financial intermediaries that would be best suited to engage in such investments, namely, life insurance companies. The potential gains, particularly to early entrants, are so great that it would be worth incurring extremely heavy administrative costs.[10]

Whatever the reason, an imperfection of the market has led to underinvestment in human capital. Government intervention might therefore be rationalized on grounds both of "technical monopoly," insofar as the obstacle to the development of such investment has been administrative costs, and of improving the operation of the market, insofar as it has been simply market frictions and rigidities.

If government does intervene, how should it do so? One obvious form of intervention, and the only form that has so far been taken, is outright government subsidy of vocational or professional schooling financed out of general revenues. This form seems clearly inappropriate. Investment should be carried to the point at which the extra return repays the investment and yields the market rate of interest on it. If the investment is in a human being, the extra return takes the form of a higher payment for the individual's services than he could otherwise command. In a private market economy, the individual would get this return as his personal income. If the investment were subsidized, he would have borne none of the costs. In consequence, if subsidies were given to all who wished

[10] It is amusing to speculate on how the business could be done and on some ancillary methods of profiting from it. The initial entrants would be able to choose the very best investments, by imposing very high quality standards on the individuals they were willing to finance. If they did so, they would increase the profitability of their investment by getting public recognition of the superior quality of the individuals they financed: the legend, "Training financed by XYZ Insurance Company" could be made into an assurance of quality (like "Approved by Good Housekeeping") that would attract custom. All sorts of other common services might be rendered by the XYZ company to "its" physicians, lawyers, dentists, and so on.

to get the training, and could meet minimum quality standards, there would tend to be overinvestment in human beings, since individuals would have an incentive to get the training so long as it yielded any extra return over private costs, even if the return were insufficient to repay the capital invested, let alone yield any interest on it. To avoid such overinvestment, government would have to restrict the subsidies. Even apart from the difficulty of calculating the "correct" amount of investment, this would involve rationing in some essentially arbitrary way the limited amount of investment among more claimants than could be financed. Those fortunate enough to get their training subsidized would receive all the returns from the investment whereas the costs would be borne by the taxpayers in general — an entirely arbitrary and almost surely perverse redistribution of income.

The desideratum is not to redistribute income but to make capital available at comparable terms for human and physical investment. Individuals should bear the costs of investment in themselves and receive the rewards. They should not be prevented by market imperfections from making the investment when they are willing to bear the costs. One way to achieve this result is for government to engage in equity investment in human beings. A governmental body could offer to finance or help finance the training of any individual who could meet minimum quality standards. It would make available a limited sum per year for a specified number of years, provided the funds were spent on securing training at a recognized institution. The individual in return would agree to pay to the government in each future year a specified percentage of his earnings in excess of a specified sum for each $1,000 that he received from the government. This payment could easily be combined with payment of income tax and so involve a minimum of additional administrative expense. The base sum should be set equal to estimated average earnings without the specialized training; the fraction of earnings paid should be calculated so as to make the whole project self-financing. In this way, the individuals who received the training would in effect bear the whole cost. The amount invested could then be determined by individual choice. Provided this was the only way in which government financed vocational or professional training, and provided the calculated earnings reflected all relevant returns and costs, the free choice of individuals would tend to produce the optimum amount of investment.

The second proviso is unfortunately not likely to be fully satisfied because of the impossibility of including non-pecuniary returns mentioned above. In practice, therefore, investment under the plan would still be somewhat too small and would not be distributed in the optimum manner.[11]

For several reasons, it would be preferable for private financial institutions and non-profit institutions such as foundations and universities to develop this plan. Because of the difficulties involved in estimating the base earnings and the fraction of earnings in excess of the base to be paid to the government, there is great danger that the scheme would turn into a political football. Information on existing earnings in various occupations would provide only a rough approximation to the values that would render the project self-financing. In addition, the base earnings and the fraction should vary from individual to individual in accordance with any differences in expected earning capacity that can be predicted in advance, just as life insurance premiums vary among groups that have different life expectancy.

Insofar as administrative expense is the obstacle to the development of such a plan on a private basis, the appropriate unit of government to make funds available is the federal government rather than smaller units. Any one state would have the same costs as an insurance company, say, in keeping track of the people whom it had financed. These would be minimized though not completely eliminated for the federal government. An individual who migrated to another country, for example, might still be legally or morally obligated to pay the agreed-on share of his earnings, yet it might be difficult and expensive to enforce the obligation. Highly successful people might therefore have an incentive to migrate. A similar

[11] I am indebted to Harry G. Johnson and Paul W. Cook, Jr., for suggesting the inclusion of this qualification. For a fuller discussion of the role of non-pecuniary advantages and disadvantages in determining earnings in different pursuits, see Friedman and Kuznets, *loc. cit.*

problem arises, of course, under the income tax, and to a very much greater extent. This and other administrative problems of conducting the scheme on a federal level, while doubtless troublesome in detail, do not seem serious. The serious problem is the political one already mentioned: how to prevent the scheme from becoming a political football and in the process being converted from a self-financing project to a means of subsidizing vocational education.

But if the danger is real, so is the opportunity. Existing imperfections in the capital market tend to restrict the more expensive vocational and professional training to individuals whose parents or benefactors can finance the training required. They make such individuals a "non-competing" group sheltered from competition by the unavailability of the necessary capital to many able individuals. The result is to perpetuate inequalities in wealth and status. The development of arrangements such as those outlined above would make capital more widely available and would thereby do much to make equality of opportunity a reality, to diminish inequalities of income and wealth, and to promote the full use of our human resources. And it would do so not by impeding competition, destroying incentive, and dealing with symptoms, as would result from the outright redistribution of income, but by strengthening competition, making incentives effective, and eliminating the causes of inequality.

Chapter VII

Capitalism and Discrimination

IT IS A STRIKING HISTORICAL FACT that the development of capitalism has been accompanied by a major reduction in the extent to which particular religious, racial, or social groups have operated under special handicaps in respect of their economic activities; have, as the saying goes, been discriminated against. The substitution of contract arrangements for status arrangements was the first step toward the freeing of the serfs in the Middle Ages. The preservation of Jews through the Middle Ages was possible because of the existence of a market sector in which they could operate and maintain themselves despite official persecution. Puritans and Quakers were able to migrate to the New World because they could accumulate the funds to do so in the market despite disabilities imposed on them in other aspects of their life. The Southern states after the Civil War took many measures to impose legal restrictions on Negroes. One measure which was never taken on any scale was the establishment of barriers to the ownership of either real or personal property. The failure to impose such barriers clearly did not reflect any special concern to avoid restrictions on Negroes. It reflected rather, a basic belief in private property which was so strong that it overrode the desire to discriminate against Negroes. The maintenance of the general rules of private property and of capitalism have been a major source of opportunity for Negroes and have permitted them to make greater progress than they otherwise could have made. To take a more general example, the preserves of discrimination in any society are the areas that are most monopolistic in character, whereas discrimination against groups of particular color or religion is least in those areas where there is the greatest freedom of competition.

As pointed out in chapter i, one of the paradoxes of experience is that, in spite of this historical evidence, it is precisely the minority groups that have frequently furnished the most vocal and most numerous advocates of fundamental alterations in a capitalist society. They have tended to attribute to capitalism the residual restrictions they experience rather than to recognize that the free market has been the major factor enabling these restrictions to be as small as they are.

We have already seen how a free market separates economic efficiency from irrelevant characteristics. As noted in chapter i, the purchaser of bread does not know whether it was made from wheat grown by a white man or a Negro, by a Christian or a Jew. In consequence, the producer of wheat is in a position to use resources as effectively as he can, regardless of what the attitudes of the community may be toward the color, the religion, or other characteristics of the people he hires. Furthermore, and perhaps more important, there is an economic incentive in a free market to separate economic efficiency from other characteristics of the individual. A businessman or an entrepreneur who expresses preferences in his business activities that are not related to productive efficiency is at a disadvantage compared to other individuals who do not. Such an individual is in effect imposing higher costs on himself than are other individuals who do not have such preferences. Hence, in a free market they will tend to drive him out.

This same phenomenon is of much wider scope. It is often taken for granted that the person who discriminates against others because of their race, religion, color, or whatever, incurs no costs by doing so but simply imposes costs on others. This view is on a par with the very similar fallacy that a country does not hurt itself by imposing tariffs on the products of other countries.[1] Both are equally wrong. The man who objects to buying from or working alongside a Negro, for example, thereby limits his range of choice. He will generally have to pay a higher price for what he buys or receive a lower return for his work. Or, put the other way, those of us who regard color of skin or religion as irrelevant can buy some things more cheaply as a result.

As these comments perhaps suggest, there are real problems in defining and interpreting discrimination. The man who exercises discrimination pays a price for doing so. He is, as it were, "buying" what he regards as a "product." It is hard to see that discrimination can have any meaning other than a "taste" of others that one does not share. We do not regard it as "discrimination"—or at least not in the same invidious sense—if an individual is willing to pay a higher price to listen to one singer than to another, although we do if he is willing to pay a higher price to have services rendered to him by a person of one color than by a person of another. The difference between the two cases is that in the one case we share the taste, and in the other case we do not. Is there any difference in principle between the taste that leads a householder to prefer an attractive servant to an ugly one and the taste that leads another to prefer a Negro to a white or a white to a Negro, except that we sympathize and agree with the one taste and may not with the other? I do not mean to say that all tastes are equally good.

[1] In a brilliant and penetrating analysis of some economic issues involved in discrimination, Gary Becker demonstrates that the problem of discrimination is almost identical in its logical structure with that of foreign trade and tariffs. See G. S. Becker, *The Economics of Discrimination* (Chicago: University of Chicago Press, 1957).

On the contrary, I believe strongly that the color of a man's skin or the religion of his parents is, by itself, no reason to treat him differently; that a man should be judged by what he is and what he does and not by these external characteristics. I deplore what seem to me the prejudice and narrowness of outlook of those whose tastes differ from mine in this respect and I think the less of them for it. But in a society based on free discussion, the appropriate recourse is for me to seek to persuade them that their tastes are bad and that they should change their views and their behavior, not to use coercive power to enforce my tastes and my attitudes on others.

FAIR EMPLOYMENT PRACTICES LEGISLATION

Fair employment practice commissions that have the task of preventing "discrimination" in employment by reason of race, color, or religion have been established in a number of states. Such legislation clearly involves interference with the freedom of individuals to enter into voluntary contracts with one another. It subjects any such contract to approval or disapproval by the state. Thus it is directly an interference with freedom of the kind that we would object to in most other contexts. Moreover, as is true with most other interferences with freedom, the individuals subjected to the law may well not be those whose actions even the proponents of the law wish to control.

For example, consider a situation in which there are grocery stores serving a neighborhood inhabited by people who have a strong aversion to being waited on by Negro clerks. Suppose one of the grocery stores has a vacancy for a clerk and the first applicant qualified in other respects happens to be a Negro. Let us suppose that as a result of the law the store is required to hire him. The effect of this action will be to reduce the business done by this store and to impose losses on the owner. If the preference of the community is strong enough, it may even cause the store to close. When the owner of the store hires white clerks in preference to Negroes in the absence of the law, he may not be expressing any preference or prejudice or taste of his own. He may simply be transmitting the tastes of the community. He is, as it were, producing the services for the consumers that the consumers are willing to pay for. Nonetheless, he is harmed, and indeed may be the only one harmed appreciably, by a law which prohibits him from engaging in this activity, that is, prohibits him from pandering to the tastes of the community for having a white rather than a Negro clerk. The consumers, whose preferences the law is intended to curb, will be affected substantially only to the extent that the number of stores is limited and hence they must pay higher prices because one store has gone out of business. This analysis can be generalized. In a very large fraction of cases, employers are transmitting the preference of either their customers or their other employees when they adopt employment policies that treat factors irrelevant to technical physical productivity as relevant to employment. Indeed, employers typically have an incentive, as noted earlier, to try to find ways of getting around the preferences of their consumers or of their employees if such preferences impose higher costs upon them.

The proponents of FEPC argue that interference with the freedom of individuals to enter into contracts with one another with respect to employment is justified because the individual who refuses to hire a Negro instead of a white, when both are equally qualified in terms of physical productive capacity, is harming others, namely, the particular color or religious group whose employment opportunity is limited in the process. This argument involves a serious confusion between two very different kinds of harm. One kind is the positive harm that one individual does another by physical force, or by forcing him to enter into a contract without his consent. An obvious example is the man who hits another over the head with a blackjack. A less obvious example is stream pollution discussed in chapter ii. The second kind is the negative harm that occurs when two individuals are unable to find mutually acceptable contracts, as when I am unwilling to buy something that someone wants to sell me and therefore make him worse off than he would be if I bought the item. If the community at large has a preference for blues singers rather than for opera singers, they are certainly increasing the economic well-being of the first relative to the second. If a potential blues singer can find employment and a potential opera singer cannot, this simply means that the blues singer is rendering services which the community regards as worth paying for whereas the potential opera singer is not. The potential opera singer is "harmed" by the community's taste. He would be better off and the blues singer "harmed" if the tastes were the reverse. Clearly, this kind of harm does not involve any involuntary exchange or an imposition of costs or granting of benefits to third parties. There is a strong case for using government to prevent one person from imposing positive harm, which is to say, to prevent coercion. There is no case whatsoever for using government to avoid the negative kind of "harm." On the contrary, such government intervention reduces freedom and limits voluntary co-operation.

FEPC legislation involves the acceptance of a principle that proponents would find abhorrent in almost every other application. If it is appropriate for the state to say that individuals may not discriminate in employment because of color or race or religion, then it is equally appropriate for the state, provided a majority can be found to vote that way, to say that individuals must discriminate in employment on the basis of color, race or religion. The Hitler Nuremberg laws and the laws in the Southern states imposing special disabilities upon Negroes are both examples of laws similar in principle to FEPC. Opponents of such laws who are in favor of FEPC cannot argue that there is anything wrong with them in principle, that they involve a kind of state action that ought not to be permitted. They can only argue that the particular criteria used are irrelevant. They can only seek to persuade other men that they should use other criteria instead of these.

If one takes a broad sweep of history and looks at the kind of things that the majority will be persuaded of if each individual case is to be decided on its merits rather than as part of a general principle, there can be little doubt that the effect of a widespread acceptance of the appropriateness of government action in this area would be extremely undesirable, even from the point of view of those who at the moment favor FEPC. If, at the moment, the proponents of FEPC are in a position to make their views effective, it is only because of a constitutional and federal situation in which a regional majority in one part of the country may be in a position to impose its views on a majority in another part of the country.

As a general rule, any minority that counts on specific majority action to defend its interests is short-sighted in the extreme. Acceptance of a general self-denying ordinance applying to a class of cases may inhibit specific majorities from exploiting specific minorities. In the absence of such a self-denying ordinance, majorities can surely be counted on to use their power to give effect to their preferences, or if you will, prejudices, not to protect minorities from the prejudices of majorities.

To put the matter in another and perhaps more striking way, consider an individual who believes that the present pattern of tastes is undesirable and who believes that Negroes have less opportunity than he would like to see them have. Suppose he puts his beliefs into practice by always choosing the Negro applicant for a job whenever there are a number of applicants more or less equally qualified in other respects. Under present circumstances should he be prevented from doing so? Clearly the logic of the FEPC is that he should be.

The counterpart to fair employment in the area where these principles have perhaps been worked out more than any other, namely, the area of speech, is "fair speech" rather than free speech. In this respect the position of the American Civil Liberties Union seems utterly contradictory. It favors both free speech and fair employment laws. One way to state the justification for free speech is that we do not believe that it is desirable that momentary majorities decide what at any moment shall be regarded as appropriate speech. We want a free market in ideas, so that ideas get a chance to win majority or near-unanimous acceptance, even if initially held only by a few. Precisely the same considerations apply to employment or more generally to the market for goods and services. Is it any more desirable that momentary majorities decide what characteristics are relevant to employment than what speech is appropriate? Indeed, can a free market in ideas long be maintained if a free market in goods and services is destroyed? The

ACLU will fight to the death to protect the right of a racist to preach on a street corner the doctrine of racial segregation. But it will favor putting him in jail if he acts on his principles by refusing to hire a Negro for a particular job.

As already stressed, the appropriate recourse of those of us who believe that a particular criterion such as color is irrelevant is to persuade our fellows to be of like mind, not to use the coercive power of the state to force them to act in accordance with our principles. Of all groups, the ACLU should be the first both to recognize and proclaim that this is so.

RIGHT-TO-WORK LAWS

Some states have passed so-called "right-to-work" laws. These are laws which make it illegal to require membership in a union as a condition of employment.

The principles involved in right-to-work laws are identical with those involved in FEPC. Both interfere with the freedom of the employment contract, in the one case by specifying that a particular color or religion cannot be made a condition of employment; in the other, that membership in a union cannot be. Despite the identity of principle, there is almost 100 per cent divergence of views with respect to the two laws. Almost all who favor FEPC oppose right to work; almost all who favor right to work oppose FEPC. As a liberal, I am opposed to both, as I am equally to laws outlawing the so-called "yellow-dog" contract (a contract making non-membership in a union a condition of employment).

Given competition among employers and employees, there seems no reason why employers should not be free to offer any terms they want to their employees. In some cases employers find that employees prefer to have part of their remuneration take the form of amenities such as baseball fields or play facilities or better rest facilities rather than cash. Employers then find that it is more profitable to offer these facilities as part of their employment contract rather than to offer higher cash wages. Similarly, employers may offer pension plans, or require participation in pension plans, and the like. None of this involves any interference with the freedom of individuals to find employment. It simply reflects an attempt by employers to make the characteristics of the job suitable and attractive to employees. So long as there are many employers, all employees who have particular kinds of wants will be able to satisfy them by finding employment with corresponding employers. Under competitive conditions the same thing would be true with respect to the closed shop. If in fact some employees would prefer to work in firms that have a closed shop and others in firms that have an open shop, there would develop different forms of employment contracts, some having the one provision, others the other provision.

As a practical matter, of course, there are some important differences between FEPC and right to work. The differences are the presence of monopoly in the form of union organizations on the employee side and the presence of federal legislation in respect of labor unions. It is doubtful that in a competitive labor market, it would in fact ever be profitable for employers to offer a closed shop as a condition of employment. Whereas unions may frequently be found without any strong monopoly power on the side of labor, a closed shop almost never is. It is almost always a symbol of monopoly power.

The coincidence of a closed shop and labor monopoly is not an argument for a right-to-work law. It is an argument for action to eliminate monopoly power regardless of the particular forms and manifestations which it takes. It is an argument for more effective and widespread antitrust action in the labor field.

Another special feature that is important in practice is the conflict between federal and state law and the existence at the moment of a federal law which applies to all the states and which leaves a loophole for the individual state only through the passage of a right-to-work law. The optimum solution would be to have the federal law revised. The difficulty is that no individual state is in a position to bring this about and yet people within an individual state might wish to have a change in the legislation governing union organization within their state. The right-to-work law may be the only effective way in which this can be done and therefore the lesser of evils. Partly,

I suppose, because I am inclined to believe that a right-to-work law will not in and of itself have any great effect on the monopoly power of the unions, I do not accept this justification for it. The practical arguments seem to me much too weak to outweigh the objection of principle.

SEGREGATION IN SCHOOLING

Segregation in schooling raises a particular problem not covered by the previous comments for one reason only. The reason is that schooling is, under present circumstances, primarily operated and administered by government. This means that government must make an explicit decision. It must either enforce segregation or enforce integration. Both seem to me bad solutions. Those of us who believe that color of skin is an irrelevant characteristic and that it is desirable for all to recognize this, yet who also believe in individual freedom, are therefore faced with a dilemma. If one must choose between the evils of enforced segregation or enforced integration, I myself would find it impossible not to choose integration.

The preceding chapter, written initially without any regard at all to the problem of segregation or integration, gives the appropriate solution that permits the avoidance of both evils — a nice illustration of how arrangements designed to enhance freedom in general cope with problems of freedom in particular. The appropriate solution is to eliminate government operation of the schools and permit parents to choose the kind of school they want their children to attend. In addition, of course, we should all of us, insofar as we possibly can, try by behavior and speech to foster the growth of attitudes and opinions that would lead mixed schools to become the rule and segregated schools the rare exception.

If a proposal like that of the preceding chapter were adopted, it would permit a variety of schools to develop, some all white, some all Negro, some mixed. It would permit the transition from one collection of schools to another — hopefully to mixed schools — to be gradual as community attitudes changed. It would avoid the harsh political conflict that has been doing so much to raise social tensions and disrupt the community. It would in this special area, as the market does in general, permit co-operation without conformity.[2]

The state of Virginia has adopted a plan having many features in common with that outlined in the preceding chapter. Though adopted for the purpose of avoiding compulsory integration, I predict that the ultimate effects of the law will be very different—after all, the difference between result and intention is one of the primary justifications of a free society; it is desirable to let men follow the bent of their own interests because there is no way of predicting where they will come out. Indeed, even in the early stages there have been surprises. I have been told that one of the first requests for a voucher to finance a change of school was by a parent transferring a child from a segregated to an integrated school. The transfer was requested not for this purpose but simply because the integrated school happened to be the better school educationally. Looking further ahead, if the voucher system is not abolished, Virginia will provide an experiment to test the conclusions of the preceding chapter. If those conclusions are right, we should see a flowering of the schools available in Virginia, with an increase in their diversity, a substantial if not spectacular rise in the quality of the leading schools, and a later rise in the quality of the rest under the impetus of the leaders.

On the other side of the picture, we should not be so naïve as to suppose that deep-seated values and beliefs can be uprooted in short measure by law. I live in Chicago. Chicago has no law compelling segregation. Its laws require integration. Yet in fact the public schools of Chicago are probably as thoroughly segregated as the schools of most Southern cities. There is almost no doubt at all that if the Virginia system were introduced in Chicago, the result would be an appreciable decrease in segregation, and a great widening in the opportunities available to the ablest and most ambitious Negro youth.

[2] To avoid misunderstanding, it should be noted explicitly that in speaking of the proposal in the preceding chapter, I am taking it for granted that the minimum requirements imposed on schools in order that vouchers be usable do not include whether the school is segregated or not.

Chapter VIII

Monopoly and the
Social Responsibility
of Business and Labor

COMPETITION HAS TWO very different meanings. In ordinary discourse, competition means personal rivalry, with one individual seeking to outdo his known competitor. In the economic world, competition means almost the opposite. There is no personal rivalry in the competitive market place. There is no personal higgling. The wheat farmer in a free market does not feel himself in personal rivalry with, or threatened by, his neighbor, who is, in fact, his competitor. The essence of a competitive market is its impersonal character. No one participant can determine the terms on which other participants shall have access to goods or jobs. All take prices as given by the market and no individual can by himself have more than a negligible influence on price though all participants together determine price by the combined effect of their separate actions.

Monopoly exists when a specific individual or enterprise has sufficient control over a particular product or service to determine significantly the terms on which other individuals shall have access to it. In some ways, monopoly comes closer to the ordinary concept of competition since it does involve personal rivalry.

Monopoly raises two classes of problems for a free society. First, the existence of monopoly means a limitation on voluntary exchange through a reduction in the alternatives available to individuals. Second, the existence of monopoly raises the issue of the "social responsibility," as it has come to be called, of the monopolist. The participant in a competitive market has no appreciable power to alter terms of exchange; he is hardly visible as a separate entity; hence it is hard to argue that he has any "social responsibility" except that which is shared by all citizens to obey the law of the land and to live according to his lights. The monopolist is visible and has power. It is easy to argue that he should discharge his power not solely to further his own interests but to further socially desirable ends. Yet the widespread application of such a doctrine would destroy a free society.

Of course, competition is an ideal type, like a Euclidean line or point. No one has ever seen a Euclidean line — which has zero width and depth — yet we all find it useful to regard many a Euclidean volume — such as a surveyor's string — as a Euclidean line. Similarly, there is no such thing as "pure" competition. Every producer has some effect, however tiny, on the price of the product he produces. The important issue for understanding and for policy is whether this effect is significant or can properly be neglected, as the surveyor can neglect the thickness of what he calls a "line." The answer must, of course, depend on the problem. But as I have studied economic activities in the United States, I have become increasingly impressed with how wide is the range of problems and industries for which it is appropriate to treat the economy as if it were competitive.

The issues raised by monopoly are technical and cover a field in which I have no special competence. In consequence, this chapter is limited to a fairly cursory survey of some of the broader issues: the extent of monopoly, sources of monopoly, appropriate government policy, and the social responsibility of business and labor.

THE EXTENT OF MONOPOLY

There are three important areas of monopoly requiring separate consideration: monopoly in industry, monopoly in labor, and governmentally produced monopoly.

1. *Monopoly in Industry* The most important fact about enterprise monopoly is its relative unimportance from the point of view of the economy as a whole. There are some four million separate operating enterprises in the United States; some four hundred thousand new ones are born each year; a somewhat smaller number die each year. Nearly one fifth of the working population is self-employed. In almost any industry that one can mention, there are giants and pygmies side by side.

Beyond these general impressions, it is difficult to cite a satisfactory objective measure of the extent of monopoly and of competition. The main reason is one already noted: these concepts as used in economic theory are ideal constructs designed to analyze particular problems rather than to describe existing situations. As a result, there can be no clear-cut determination of whether a particular enterprise or industry is to be regarded as monopolistic or as competitive. The difficulty of assigning precise meanings to such terms leads to much misunderstanding. The same word is used to refer to different things, depending on the background of experience in terms of which the state of competition is judged. Perhaps the most striking example is the extent to which an American student will describe as monopolistic, arrangements that a European would regard as highly competitive. As a result, Europeans interpreting American literature and discussion in terms of the meaning attached to the terms competition and monopoly in Europe tend to believe that there is a much greater degree of monopoly in the United States than in fact exists.

A number of studies, particularly by G. Warren Nutter and

George J. Stigler, have tried to classify industries as monopolistic, workably competitive, and governmentally operated or supervised, and to trace changes over time in these categories.[1] They conclude that, as of 1939, roughly one quarter of the economy could be regarded as governmentally operated or supervised. Of the three-quarters remaining, at most one-quarter and perhaps as little as 15 per cent can be regarded as monopolistic, at least three-quarters and perhaps as much as 85 per cent, as competitive. The governmentally operated or supervised sector has of course grown greatly over the past half-century or so. Within the private sector, on the other hand, there appears not to have been any tendency for the scope of monopoly to have increased and it may well have decreased.

There is, I suspect, a widespread impression that monopoly is both far more important than these estimates suggest and has been growing steadily over time. One reason for this mistaken impression is the tendency to confuse absolute and relative size. As the economy has grown, enterprises have become larger in absolute size. This has been taken to mean also that they account for a larger fraction of the market, whereas the market may have grown even faster. A second reason is that monopoly is more newsworthy and leads to more attention than competition. If individuals were asked to list the major industries in the United States, almost all would include automobile production, few would include wholesale trade. Yet wholesale trade is twice as important as automobile production. Wholesale trade is highly competitive, hence draws little attention to itself. Few people could name any leading enterprises in wholesale trade, though there are some that are very large in absolute size. Automobile production, while in certain respects highly competitive, has many fewer firms and is certainly closer to monopoly. Everyone can name the leading firms producing automobiles. To cite one other striking example: domestic service is a vastly more important industry than the telegraph and telephone industry. A third reason is the general bias and tendency to overemphasize

[1] G. Warren Nutter, *The Extent of Enterprise Monopoly in the United States, 1899–1939* (Chicago: University of Chicago Press, 1951) and George J. Stigler, *Five Lectures on Economic Problems* (London; Longmans, Green and Co., 1949), pp. 46–65.

the importance of the big versus the small, of which the preceding point is only a particular manifestation. Finally, the main characteristic of our society is taken to be its industrial character. This leads to overemphasis of the manufacturing sector of the economy, which accounts for only about one-quarter of output or employment. And monopoly is far more prevalent in manufacturing than in other sectors of the economy.

The over-estimation of the importance of monopoly is accompanied, for much the same reasons, by an over-estimation of the importance of those technological changes that promote monopoly by comparison with those that extend competition. For example, the spread of mass production has been greatly stressed. The developments in transportation and communication that have promoted competition by reducing the importance of local regional markets and widening the scope within which competition could take place have been given much less attention. The growing concentration of the automobile industry is a commonplace; growth of the trucking industry which reduces dependence on large railroads passes with little notice; so does the declining concentration in the steel industry.

2. *Monopoly in Labor*   There is a similar tendency to overestimate the importance of monopoly on the side of labor. Labor unions include roughly a quarter of the working population and this greatly overestimates the importance of unions on the structure of wages. Many unions are utterly ineffective. Even the strong and powerful unions have only a limited effect on the wage structure. It is even clearer for labor than for industry why there is a strong tendency to overestimate the importance of monopoly. Given a labor union, any wage increase will come through the union, even though it may not be a consequence of the union organization. The wages of domestic servants have risen very greatly in recent years. Had there been a union of domestic servants, the increase would have come through the union and would have been attributed to it.

This is not to say that unions are unimportant. Like enterprise monopoly, they play a significant and meaningful role making many wage rates different from what the market alone would establish. It would be as much a mistake to underestimate as to overestimate their importance. I once made a rough estimate that because of unions something like 10 to 15 per cent of the working population has had its wage rates raised by something like 10 to 15 per cent. This means that something like 85 or 90 per cent of the working population has had its wage rates reduced by some 4 per cent.[2] Since I made these estimates, much more detailed studies have been done by others. My impression is that they yield results of much the same order of magnitude.

If unions raise wage rates in a particular occupation or industry, they necessarily make the amount of employment available in that occupation or industry less than it otherwise would be — just as any higher price cuts down the amount purchased. The effect is an increased number of persons seeking other jobs, which forces down wages in other occupations. Since unions have generally been strongest among groups that would have been high-paid anyway, their effect has been to make high-paid workers higher paid at the expense of lower-paid workers. Unions have therefore not only harmed the public at large and workers as a whole by distorting the use of labor; they have also made the incomes of the working class more unequal by reducing the opportunities available to the most disadvantaged workers.

In one respect, there is an important difference between labor and enterprise monopoly. While there seems not to have been any upward trend in the importance of enterprise monopoly over the past half-century, there certainly has been in the importance of labor monopoly. Labor unions grew notably in importance during World War I, declined during the 'twenties and early 'thirties, then took an enormous leap forward during the New Deal period. They consolidated their gains during and after World War II. More recently, they have been just holding their own or even declining. The decline does not reflect a decline within particular industries or occupations but rather a declining importance of those industries or occupations in which unions are strong relative to those in which unions are weak.

[2] "Some Comments on the Significance of Labor Unions for Economic Policy," in David McCord Wright (ed.), *The Impact of the Union* (New York: Harcourt, Brace, 1951), pp. 204–34.

The distinction I have been drawing between labor monopoly and enterprise monopoly is in one respect too sharp. To some extent, labor unions have served as a means of enforcing monopoly in the sale of a product. The clearest example is in coal. The Guffey Coal Act was an attempt to provide legal support for a price-fixing cartel of coal-mine operators. When, in the mid-thirties, this Act was declared unconstitutional, John L. Lewis and the United Mine Workers stepped into the breach. By calling strikes or work stoppages whenever the amount of coal above the ground got so large as to threaten to force down prices, Lewis controlled output and thereby prices with the unspoken co-operation of the industry. The gains from this cartel management were divided between the coal mine operators and the miners. The gain to the miners was in the form of higher wage rates, which of course meant fewer miners employed. Hence only those miners who retained employment shared the cartel gains and even they took a large part of the gain in the form of greater leisure. The possibility of the unions playing this role derives from their exemption from the Sherman Antitrust Act. Many other unions have taken advantage of this exemption and are better interpreted as enterprises selling the services of cartellizing an industry than as labor organizations. The Teamster's Union is perhaps the most notable.

3. *Government and Government-Supported Monopoly* In the United States, direct government monopoly in the production of goods for sale is not very extensive. The post office, electric power production, as by TVA and other publicly owned power stations; the provision of highway services, sold indirectly through the gasoline tax or directly by tolls, and municipal water and similar plants are the main examples. In addition, with so large a defense, space, and research budget as we now have, the federal government has become essentially the only purchaser of the products of many enterprises and whole industries. This raises very serious problems for the preservation of a free society, but not of a kind that are best considered under the heading of "monopoly."

The use of government to establish, support and enforce cartel and monopoly arrangements among private producers has grown much more rapidly than direct government monopoly and is currently far more important. The Interstate Commerce Commission is an early example, and it has extended its scope from railroads to trucking and other means of transport. The agricultural program is undoubtedly the most notorious. It is essentially a governmentally enforced cartel. Other examples are the Federal Communications Commission, with its control over radio and television; the Federal Power Commission, with its control over oil and gas moving in interstate trade; the Civil Aeronautics Board, with its control over airlines; and the enforcement by the Federal Reserve Board of maximum interest rates that banks may pay on time deposits, and the legal prohibition of the payment of interest on demand deposits.

These examples are on a federal level. In addition, there has been a great proliferation of similar developments on a state and local level. The Texas Railroad Commission, which so far as I know, has nothing to do with railroads, enforces output restrictions on oil wells, by limiting the number of days when wells may produce. It does so in the name of conservation but in fact for the purpose of controlling prices. More recently, it has been strongly assisted by federal import quotas on oil. Keeping oil wells idle most of the time to keep up prices seems to me featherbedding of precisely the same kind as paying coal firemen on diesel locomotives for being idle. Yet some representatives of business who are loudest in their condemnation of labor featherbedding as a violation of free enterprise — notably the oil industry itself — are deafeningly silent about featherbedding in oil.

Licensure provisions, discussed in the next chapter, are another example of governmentally created and supported monopoly on a state level. Restrictions on the number of taxicabs that can be operated exemplify similar restriction on a local level. In New York, a medallion signifying the right to operate an independent cab now sells for something like $20,000 to $25,-000; in Philadelphia, for $15,000. Another example on a local level is the enactment of building codes, ostensibly designed for public safety, but in fact generally under the control of local building trade unions or associations of private contractors. Such restrictions are numerous and apply to a considerable variety of activities on both city and state levels. All constitute arbitrary limitations on the ability of individuals to enter into voluntary exchanges with one another. They simultaneously restrict freedom and promote the waste of resources.

A kind of governmentally created monopoly very different in principle from those so far considered is the grant of patents to inventors and copyrights to authors. These are different, because they can equally be regarded as defining property rights. In a literal sense, if I have a property right to a particular piece of land, I can be said to have a monopoly with respect to that piece of land defined and enforced by the government. With respect to inventions and publications, the problem is whether it is desirable to establish an analogous property right. This problem is part of the general need to use government to establish what shall and what shall not be regarded as property.

In both patents and copyrights, there is clearly a strong prima facie case for establishing property rights. Unless this is done, the inventor will find it difficult or impossible to collect a payment for the contribution his invention makes to output. He will, that is, confer benefits on others for which he cannot be compensated. Hence he will have no incentive to devote the time and effort required to produce the invention. Similar considerations apply to the writer.

At the same time, there are costs involved. For one thing, there are many "inventions" that are not patentable. The "inventor" of the supermarket, for example, conferred great benefits on his fellowmen for which he could not charge them. Insofar as the same kind of ability is required for the one kind of invention as for the other, the existence of patents tends to divert activity to patentable inventions. For another, trivial patents, or patents that would be of dubious legality if contested in court, are often used as a device for maintaining private collusive arrangements that would otherwise be more difficult or impossible to maintain.

These are very superficial comments on a difficult and important problem. Their aim is not to suggest any specific answer but only to show why patents and copyrights are in a different class from the other governmentally supported monopolies and to illustrate the problem of social policy that they raise. One

128 CAPITALISM AND FREEDOM

thing is clear. The specific conditions attached to patents and copyrights — for example, the grant of patent protection for seventeen years rather than some other period — are not a matter of principle. They are matters of expediency to be determined by practical considerations. I am myself inclined to believe that a much shorter period of patent protection would be preferable. But this is a casual judgment on a subject on which there has been much detailed study and on which much more is needed. Hence, it is deserving of little confidence.

THE SOURCES OF MONOPOLY

There are three major sources of monopoly: "technical" considerations, direct and indirect governmental assistance, and private collusion.

1. *Technical Considerations* As pointed out in chapter ii, monopoly arises to some extent because technical considerations make it more efficient or economical to have a single enterprise rather than many. The most obvious example is a telephone system, water system, and the like in an individual community. There is unfortunately no good solution for technical monopoly. There is only a choice among three evils: private unregulated monopoly, private monopoly regulated by the state, and government operation.

It seems impossible to state as a general proposition that one of these evils is uniformly preferable to another. As stated in chapter ii, the great disadvantage of either governmental regulation or governmental operation of monopoly is that it is exceedingly difficult to reverse. In consequence, I am inclined to urge that the least of the evils is private unregulated monopoly wherever this is tolerable. Dynamic changes are highly likely to undermine it and there is at least some chance that these will be allowed to have their effect. And even in the short run, there is generally a wider range of substitutes than there seems to be at first blush, so private enterprises are fairly narrowly limited in the extent to which it is profitable to keep prices above cost. Moreover, as we have seen, the regulatory agencies often tend themselves to fall under the control of the producers and so prices may not be any lower with regulation than without regulation.

Fortunately, the areas in which technical considerations make monopoly a likely or a probable outcome are fairly limited. They would offer no serious threat to the preservation of a free economy if it were not for the tendency of regulation, introduced on this ground, to spread to situations in which it is not so justified.

2. *Direct and Indirect Government Assistance* Probably the most important source of monopoly power has been government assistance, direct and indirect. Numerous examples of reasonably direct government assistance have been cited above. The indirect assistance to monopoly consists of measures taken for other purposes which have as a largely unintended effect the imposition of limitations on potential competitors of existing firms. Perhaps the three clearest examples are tariffs, tax legislation, and law enforcement and legislation with respect to labor disputes.

Tariffs have of course been imposed largely to "protect" domestic industries, which means to impose handicaps on potential competitors. They always interfere with the freedom of individuals to engage in voluntary exchange. After all, the liberal takes the individual, not the nation or citizen of a particular nation, as his unit. Hence he regards it just as much a violation of freedom if citizens of the United States and Switzerland are prevented from consummating an exchange that would be mutually advantageous as if two citizens of the United States are prevented from doing so. Tariffs need not produce monopoly. If the market for the protected industry is sufficiently large and technical conditions permit many firms, there can be effective competition domestically in the protected industry, as in the United States in textiles. Clearly, however, tariffs do foster monopoly. It is far easier for a few firms than for many to collude to fix prices, and it is generally easier for enterprises in the same country to collude than for enterprises in different countries. Britain was protected by free trade from widespread monopoly during the nineteenth and early twentieth centuries, despite the relatively small size of her domestic market and the large scale of many firms. Monopoly has become a much more serious problem in Britain since free trade was abandoned, first after World War I and then more extensively in the early 1930's.

The effects of tax legislation have been even more indirect yet not less important. A major element has been the linkage of the corporate and individual income tax combined with the special treatment of capital gains under the individual income tax. Let us suppose a corporation earns an income of $1 million over and above corporate taxes. If it pays the whole million dollars to its stockholders as dividends, they must include it as part of their taxable income. Suppose they would, on the average, have to pay 50 per cent of this additional income as income tax. They would then have available only $500,000 to spend on consumption or to save and invest. If instead the corporation pays no cash dividends to its stockholders, it has the whole million dollars to invest internally. Such reinvestment will tend to raise the capital value of its stock. Stockholders who would have saved the funds if distributed can simply hold the stock and postpone all taxes until they sell the stock. They, as well as others who sell at an earlier date to realize income for consumption, will pay tax at capital gains rates, which are lower than rates on regular income.

This tax structure encourages retention of corporate earnings. Even if the return that can be earned internally is appreciably less than the return that the stockholder himself could earn by investing the funds externally, it may pay to invest internally because of the tax saving. This leads to a waste of capital, to its use for less productive rather than more productive purposes. It has been a major reason for the post-World-War-II tendency toward horizontal diversification as firms have sought outlets for their earnings. It is also a great source of strength for established corporations relative to new enterprises. The established corporations can be less productive than new enterprises, yet their stockholders have an incentive to invest in them rather than to have the income paid out so that they can invest it in new enterprises through the capital market.

A major source of labor monopoly has been government assistance. Licensure provisions, building codes, and the like, discussed above have been one source. Legislation granting special immunities to labor unions, such as exemption from the antitrust laws, restrictions on union responsibility, the right to appear before special tribunals, and so on, are a second source. Perhaps of equal or greater importance than either is a general climate of opinion and law enforcement applying different standards to actions taken in the course of a labor dispute than to the same actions under other circumstances. If men turn cars over, or destroy property, out of sheer wickedness or in the course of exacting private vengeance, not a hand will be lifted to protect them from the legal consequences. If they commit the same acts in the course of labor dispute, they may well get off scot free. Union actions involving actual or potential physical violence or coercion could hardly take place if it were not for the unspoken acquiescence of the authorities.

3. *Private Collusion* The final source of monopoly is private collusion. As Adam Smith says, "People of the same trade seldom meet together, even for merriment and diversion, but the conversation ends in a conspiracy against the public, or in some contrivance to raise prices."[3] Such collusion or private cartel arrangements are therefore constantly arising. However, they are generally unstable and of brief duration unless they can call government to their assistance. The establishment of the cartel, by raising prices, makes it more profitable for outsiders to enter the industry. Moreover, since the higher price can be established only by the participants' restricting their output below the level that they would like to produce at the fixed price, there is an incentive for each one separately to undercut the price in order to expand output. Each one, of course, hopes that the others will abide by the agreement. It takes only one or at most a few "chiselers" — who are indeed public benefactors — to break the cartel. In the absence of government assistance in enforcing the cartel, they are almost sure to succeed fairly promptly.

The major role of our antitrust laws has been to inhibit such private collusion. Their main contribution in this respect has been less through actual prosecutions than by their indirect effects. They have ruled out the obvious collusive devices — such

[3] *The Wealth of Nations* (1776), Bk. I, chap. x, Pt. II (Cannan ed. London, 1930), p. 130.

as the public get-together for this specific purpose — and have
therefore made collusion more expensive. More important, they
have reaffirmed common law doctrine that combinations in re-
straint of trade are unenforceable in the courts. In various European countries, the courts will enforce an agreement entered
into by a group of enterprises to sell only through a joint selling
agency, committing the enterprises to pay specified penalties if
they violate the agreement. In the United States, such an agreement would not be enforceable in the courts. This difference is
one of the major reasons why cartels have been more stable and
widespread in European countries than in the United States.

APPROPRIATE GOVERNMENT POLICY

The first and most urgent necessity in the area of government
policy is the elimination of those measures which directly support monopoly, whether enterprise monopoly or labor monopoly, and an even-handed enforcement of the laws on enterprises
and labor unions alike. Both should be subjected to the antitrust laws; both should be treated alike with respect to laws
about the destruction of property and about interference with
private activities.

Beyond this, the most important and effective step toward
the reduction of monopoly power would be an extensive reform
of the tax laws. The corporate tax should be abolished. Whether
this is done or not, corporations should be required to attribute
to individual stockholders earnings which are not paid out as
dividends. That is, when the corporation sends out a dividend
check, it should also send a statement saying, "In addition to
this dividend of ——— cents per share, your corporation also
earned ——— cents per share which was reinvested." The individual stockholder should then be required to report the attributed but undistributed earnings on his tax return as well as
the dividend. Corporations would still be free to plough back
as much as they wish, but they would have no incentive to do
so except the proper incentive that they could earn more internally than the stockholder could earn externally. Few measures would do more to invigorate capital markets, to stimulate
enterprise, and to promote effective competition.

Of course, so long as the individual income tax is as highly graduated as it is now, there is strong pressure to find devices to evade its impact. In this way as well as directly, the highly graduated income tax constitutes a serious impediment to the efficient use of our resources. The appropriate solution is the drastic scaling down of the higher rates, combined with an elimination of the avoidance devices that have been incorporated in the law.

SOCIAL RESPONSIBILITY OF BUSINESS AND LABOR

The view has been gaining widespread acceptance that corporate officials and labor leaders have a "social responsibility" that goes beyond serving the interest of their stockholders or their members. This view shows a fundamental misconception of the character and nature of a free economy. In such an economy, there is one and only one social responsibility of business — to use its resources and engage in activities designed to increase its profits so long as it stays within the rules of the game, which is to say, engages in open and free competition, without deception or fraud. Similarly, the "social responsibility" of labor leaders is to serve the interests of the members of their unions. It is the responsibility of the rest of us to establish a framework of law such that an individual in pursuing his own interest is, to quote Adam Smith again, "led by an invisible hand to promote an end which was no part of his intention. Nor is it always the worse for the society that it was no part of it. By pursuing his own interest, he frequently promotes that of the society more effectually than when he really intends to promote it. I have never known much good done by those who affected to trade for the public good."[4]

Few trends could so thoroughly undermine the very foundations of our free society as the acceptance by corporate officials of a social responsibility other than to make as much money for their stockholders as possible. This is a fundamentally subversive doctrine. If businessmen do have a social responsibility other than making maximum profits for stockholders, how are they to know what it is? Can self-selected private individuals decide what the social interest is? Can they decide how great a burden

[4] *Ibid*, Bk. IV, chapter ii, p. 421.

they are justified in placing on themselves or their stockholders to serve that social interest? Is it tolerable that these public functions of taxation, expenditure, and control be exercised by the people who happen at the moment to be in charge of particular enterprises, chosen for those posts by strictly private groups? If businessmen are civil servants rather than the employees of their stockholders then in a democracy they will, sooner or later, be chosen by the public techniques of election and appointment.

And long before this occurs, their decision-making power will have been taken away from them. A dramatic illustration was the cancellation of a steel price increase by U.S. Steel in April 1962 through the medium of a public display of anger by President Kennedy and threats of reprisals on levels ranging from anti-trust suits to examination of the tax reports of steel executives. This was a striking episode because of the public display of the vast powers concentrated in Washington. We were all made aware of how much of the power needed for a police state was already available. It illustrates the present point as well. If the price of steel is a public decision, as the doctrine of social responsibility declares, then it cannot be permitted to be made privately.

The particular aspect of the doctrine which this example illustrates, and which has been most prominent recently, is an alleged social responsibility of business and labor to keep prices and wage rates down in order to avoid price inflation. Suppose that at a time when there was upward pressure on prices — ultimately of course reflecting an increase in the stock of money — every businessman and labor leader were to accept this responsibility and suppose all could succeed in keeping any price from rising, so we had voluntary price and wage control without open inflation. What would be the result? Clearly product shortages, labor shortages, gray markets, black markets. If prices are not allowed to ration goods and workers, there must be some other means to do so. Can the alternative rationing schemes be private? Perhaps for a time in a small and unimportant area. But if the goods involved are many and important, there will necessarily be pressure, and probably irresistible pressure, for governmental rationing of goods, a governmental wage policy, and governmental measures for allocating and distributing labor.

Price controls, whether legal or voluntary, if effectively enforced would eventually lead to the destruction of the free-enterprise system and its replacement by a centrally controlled system. And it would not even be effective in preventing inflation. History offers ample evidence that what determines the average level of prices and wages is the amount of money in the economy and not the greediness of businessmen or of workers. Governments ask for the self-restraint of business and labor because of their inability to manage their own affairs — which includes the control of money — and the natural human tendency to pass the buck.

One topic in the area of social responsibility that I feel duty-bound to touch on, because it affects my own personal interests, has been the claim that business should contribute to the support of charitable activities and especially to universities. Such giving by corporations is an inappropriate use of corporate funds in a free-enterprise society.

The corporation is an instrument of the stockholders who own it. If the corporation makes a contribution, it prevents the individual stockholder from himself deciding how he should dispose of his funds. With the corporation tax and the deductibility of contributions, stockholders may of course want the corporation to make a gift on their behalf, since this would enable them to make a larger gift. The best solution would be the abolition of the corporate tax. But so long as there is a corporate tax, there is no justification for permitting deductions for contributions to charitable and educational institutions. Such contributions should be made by the individuals who are the ultimate owners of property in our society.

People who urge extension of the deductibility of this kind of corporate contribution in the name of free enterprise are fundamentally working against their own interest. A major complaint made frequently against modern business is that it involves the separation of ownership and control — that the corporation has become a social institution that is a law unto itself, with irresponsible executives who do not serve the interests of their stockholders. This charge is not true. But the direction in which policy is now moving, of permitting corporations to make contributions for charitable purposes and allowing deductions for income tax, is a step in the direction of creating a true divorce between ownership and control and of undermining the basic nature and character of our society. It is a step away from an individualistic society and toward the corporate state.

Chapter IX

Occupational Licensure

THE OVERTHROW OF the medieval guild system was an indispensable early step in the rise of freedom in the Western world. It was a sign of the triumph of liberal ideas, and widely recognized as such, that by the mid-nineteenth century, in Britain, the United States, and to a lesser extent on the continent of Europe, men could pursue whatever trade or occupation they wished without the by-your-leave of any governmental or quasi-governmental authority. In more recent decades, there has been a retrogression, an increasing tendency for particular occupations to be restricted to individuals licensed to practice them by the state.

These restrictions on the freedom of individuals to use their resources as they wish are important in their own right. In addition, they provide still a different class of problems to which we can apply the principles developed in the first two chapters.

I shall discuss first the general problem and then a particular example, restrictions on the practice of medicine. The reason for choosing medicine is that it seems desirable to discuss the restrictions for which the strongest case can be made — there is not much to be learned by knocking down straw men. I suspect that most people, possibly even most liberals, believe that it is desirable to restrict the practice of medicine to people who are licensed by the state. I agree that the case for licensure is stronger for medicine than for most other fields. Yet the conclusions I shall reach are that liberal principles do not justify licensure even in medicine and that in practice the results of state licensure in medicine have been undesirable.

Licensure is a special case of a much more general and exceedingly widespread phenomenon, namely, edicts that individuals may not engage in particular economic activities except under conditions laid down by a constituted authority of the state. Medieval guilds were a particular example of an explicit system for specifying which individuals should be permitted to follow particular pursuits. The Indian caste system is another example. To a considerable extent in the caste system, to a lesser extent in the guilds, the restrictions were enforced by general social customs rather than explicitly by government.

A widespread notion about the caste system is that every person's occupation is completely determined by the caste into which he is born. It is obvious to an economist that this is an impossible system, since it prescribes a rigid distribution of persons among occupations determined entirely by birthrates and not at all by conditions of demand. Of course, this is not the way the system worked. What was true, and to some measure still is, was that a limited number of occupations were reserved to members of certain castes, but not every member of those castes followed those occupations. There were some general occupations, such as general agricultural work, which members of various castes might engage in. These permitted an adjustment of the supply of people in different occupations to the demand for their services.

Currently, tariffs, fair-trade laws, import quotas, production quotas, trade union restrictions on employment and so on are examples of similar phenomena. In all these cases, governmental authority determines the conditions under which particular individuals can engage in particular activities, which is to say, the terms on which some individuals are permitted to make arrangements with others. The common feature of these examples, as well as of licensure, is that the legislation is enacted on behalf of a producer group. For licensure, the producer group is generally a craft. For the other examples, it may be a group producing a particular product which wants a tariff, a group of small retailers who would like to be protected from competition by the "chiseling" chain stores, or a group of oil producers, of farmers, or of steel workers.

Occupational licensure is by now very widespread. According to Walter Gellhorn, who has written the best brief survey I know, "By 1952 more than 80 separate occupations exclusive of 'owner-businesses,' like restaurants and taxicab companies, had been licensed by state law; and in addition to the state laws there are municipal ordinances in abundance, not to mention the federal statutes that require the licensing of such diverse occupations as radio operators and stockyard commission agents. As long ago as 1938 a single state, North Carolina, had extended its law to 60 occupations. One may not be surprised to learn that pharmacists, accountants, and dentists have been reached by state law as have sanitarians and psychologists, assayers and architects, veterinarians and librarians. But with what joy of discovery does one learn about the licensing of threshing machine operators and dealers in scrap tobacco? What of egg graders and guide dog trainers, pest controllers and yacht salesmen, tree surgeons and well diggers, tile layers and potato growers? And what of the hypertrichologists who are licensed in Connecticut, where they remove excessive and unsightly hair with the solemnity appropriate to their high sounding title?"[1] In the arguments that seek to persuade legislatures to enact such licensure provisions, the justification is always said to be the necessity of protecting the public interest. However, the pressure on the legislature to license an occupation rarely comes from the members of the public who have been mulcted or in other ways abused by members of the occupation. On the contrary, the pressure invariably comes from members of the occupation itself. Of course, they are more aware than others of how much they exploit the customer and so perhaps they can lay claim to expert knowledge.

Similarly, the arrangements made for licensure almost invariably involve control by members of the occupation which is to be licensed. Again, this is in some ways quite natural. If the occupation of plumbing is to be restricted to those who have the requisite capacity and skills to provide good service for their customers, clearly only plumbers are capable of judging who should be licensed. Consequently, the board or other body that grants licenses is almost invariably made up largely of plumbers or pharmacists or physicians or whatever may be the particular occupation licensed.

Gellhorn points out that "Seventy-five per cent of the occupational licensing boards at work in this country today are composed exclusively of licensed practitioners in the respective occupations. These men and women, most of whom are only part-time officials, may have a direct economic interest in many of the decisions they make concerning admission requirements and the definition of standards to be observed by licensees. More importantly, they are as a rule directly representative of organized groups within the occupations. Ordinarily they are nominated by these groups as a step toward a gubernatorial or other appointment that is frequently a mere formality. Often the formality is dispensed with entirely, appointment being made directly by the occupational association — as happens, for example, with the embalmers in North Carolina, the den-

[1] Walter Gellhorn, *Individual Freedom and Governmental Restraints* (Baton Rouge: Louisiana State University Press, 1956). Chapter entitled "The Right to Make a Living," p. 106.

tists in Alabama, the psychologists in Virginia, the physicians in Maryland, and the attorneys in Washington." [2]

Licensure therefore frequently establishes essentially the medieval guild kind of regulation in which the state assigns power to the members of the profession. In practice, the considerations taken into account in determining who shall get a license often involve matters that, so far as a layman can see, have no relation whatsoever to professional competence. This is not surprising. If a few individuals are going to decide whether other individuals may pursue an occupation, all sorts of irrelevant considerations are likely to enter. Just what the irrelevant considerations will be, will depend on the personalities of the members of the licensing board and the mood of the time. Gellhorn notes the extent to which a loyalty oath was required of various occupations when the fear of communist subversion was sweeping the country. He writes, "A Texas statute of 1952 requires each applicant for a pharmacist's license to swear that 'he is not a member of the Communist Party or affiliated with such party, and that he does not believe in and is neither a member of nor supports any group or organization that believes in, furthers or teaches the overthrow of the United States Government by force or any illegal or unconstitutional methods.' The relationship between this oath on the one hand and, on the other, the public health which is the interest purportedly protected by the licensing of pharmacists, is somewhat obscure. No more apparent is the justification for requiring professional boxers and wrestlers in Indiana to swear that they are not subversive . . . A junior high school teacher of music, having been forced to resign after being identified as a Communist, had difficulty becoming a piano tuner in the District of Columbia because, forsooth, he was 'under Communist discipline.' Veterinarians in the state of Washington may not minister to an ailing cow or cat unless they have first signed a non-Communist oath." [3]

Whatever one's attitude towards communism, any relationship between the requirements imposed and the qualities

[2] Ibid. pp. 140–41.
[3] *Ibid.*, pp. 129–30.

which the licensure is intended to assure is rather far-fetched. The extent to which such requirements go is sometimes little short of ludicrous. A few more quotations from Gellhorn may provide a touch of comic relief.[4]

One of the most amusing sets of regulations is that laid down for barbers, a trade that is licensed in many places. Here is an example from a law which was declared invalid by Maryland courts, though similar language can be found in statutes of other states which were declared legal. "The court was depressed rather than impressed by a legislative command that neophyte barbers must receive formal instruction in the 'scientific fundamentals for barbering, hygiene, bacteriology, histology of the hair, skin, nails, muscles and nerves, structure of the head, face and neck, elementary chemistry relating to sterilization and antiseptics, disease of the skin, hair, glands and nails, haircutting, shaving and arranging, dressing, coloring, bleaching, and tinting of the hair'."[5] One more quotation on the barbers: "Of eighteen representative states included in a study of barbering regulations in 1929, not one then commanded an aspirant to be a graduate of a 'barber college,' though apprenticeship was necessary in all. Today, the states typically insist upon graduation from a barbering school that provides not less (and often much more) than one thousand hours of instruction in 'theoretical subjects' such as sterilization of instruments, and this must still be followed by apprenticeship."[6] I trust these quotations make it clear that the problem of licensing of occupations is something more than a trivial illustration of the problem of state intervention, that it is already in this country a serious infringement on the freedom of individuals to pursue activities of their own choice, and that it threatens to become a much more serious one with the continual pressure upon legislatures to extend it.

Before discussing the advantages and disadvantages of licens-

[4] In fairness to Walter Gellhorn, I should note that he does not share my view that the correct solution to these problems is to abandon licensing. On the contrary, he thinks that while licensing has gone much too far it has some real functions to perform. He suggests procedural reforms and changes that in his view would limit the abuse of licensure arrangements.

[5] *Ibid.*, pp. 121–22.

[6] *Ibid.*, p. 146.

ing, it is worth noting why we have it and what general political problem is revealed by the tendency for such special legislation to be enacted. The declaration by a large number of different state legislatures that barbers must be approved by a committee of other barbers is hardly persuasive evidence that there is in fact a public interest in having such legislation. Surely the explanation is different; it is that a producer group tends to be more concentrated politically than a consumer group. This is an obvious point often made and yet one whose importance cannot be overstressed.[7] Each of us is a producer and also a consumer. However, we are much more specialized and devote a much larger fraction of our attention to our activity as a producer than as a consumer. We consume literally thousands if not millions of items. The result is that people in the same trade, like barbers or physicians, all have an intense interest in the specific problems of this trade and are willing to devote considerable energy to doing something about them. On the other hand, those of us who use barbers at all, get barbered infrequently and spend only a minor fraction of our income in barber shops. Our interest is casual. Hardly any of us are willing to devote much time going to the legislature in order to testify against the iniquity of restricting the practice of barbering. The same point holds for tariffs. The groups that think they have a special interest in particular tariffs are concentrated groups to whom the issue makes a great deal of difference. The public interest is widely dispersed. In consequence, in the absence of any general arrangements to offset the pressure of special interests, producer groups will invariably have a much stronger influence on legislative action and the powers that be than will the diverse, widely spread consumer interest. Indeed from this point of view, the puzzle is not why we have so many silly licensure laws, but why we don't have far more. The puzzle is how we ever succeeded in getting the relative freedom from government controls over the productive activities of individuals that we have had and still have in this country, and that other countries have had as well.

[7] See, for example, Wesley Mitchell's famous article on the "Backward Art of Spending Money," reprinted in his book of essays carrying that title (New York: McGraw-Hill, 1937), pp. 3–19.

The only way that I can see to offset special producer groups is to establish a general presumption against the state undertaking certain kinds of activities. Only if there is a general recognition that governmental activities should be severely limited with respect to a class of cases, can the burden of proof be put strongly enough on those who would depart from this general presumption to give a reasonable hope of limiting the spread of special measures to further special interests. This point is one we have adverted to time and again. It is of a piece with the argument for the Bill of Rights and for a rule to govern monetary policy and fiscal policy.

POLICY ISSUES RAISED BY LICENSURE

It is important to distinguish three different levels of control: first, registration; second, certification; third, licensing.

By registration, I mean an arrangement under which individuals are required to list their names in some official register if they engage in certain kinds of activities. There is no provision for denying the right to engage in the activity to anyone who is willing to list his name. He may be charged a fee, either as a registration fee or as a scheme of taxation.

The second level is certification. The governmental agency may certify that an individual has certain skills but may not prevent, in any way, the practice of any occupation using these skills by people who do not have such a certificate. One example is accountancy. In most states, anybody can be an accountant, whether he is a certified public accountant or not, but only those people who have passed a particular test can put the title CPA after their names or can put a sign in their offices saying they are certified public accountants. Certification is frequently only an intermediate stage. In many states, there has been a tendency to restrict an increasing range of activities to certified public accountants. With respect to such activities there is licensure, not certification. In some states, "architect" is a title which can be used only by those who have passed a specified examination. This is certification. It does not prevent anyone else from going into the business of advising people for a fee how to build houses.

The third stage is licensing proper. This is an arrangement under which one must obtain a license from a recognized authority in order to engage in the occupation. The license is more than a formality. It requires some demonstration of competence or the meeting of some tests ostensibly designed to insure competence, and anyone who does not have a license is not authorized to practice and is subject to a fine or a jail sentence if he does engage in practice.

The question I want to consider is this: under what circumstances, if any, can we justify the one or the other of these steps? There are three different grounds on which it seems to me registration can be justified consistently with liberal principles.

First, it may assist in the pursuit of other aims. Let me illustrate. The police are often concerned with acts of violence. After the event, it is desirable to find out who had access to firearms. Before the event, it is desirable to prevent firearms from getting into the hands of people who are likely to use them for criminal purposes. It may assist in the pursuit of this aim to register stores selling firearms. Of course, if I may revert to a point made several times in earlier chapters, it is never enough to say that there *might* be a justification along these lines, in order to conclude that there *is* justification. It is necessary to set up a balance sheet of the advantages and disadvantages in the light of liberal principles. All I am now saying is that this consideration might in some cases justify overriding the general presumption against requiring the registration of people.

Second, registration is sometimes a device to facilitate taxation and nothing more. The questions at issue then become whether the particular tax is an appropriate method to raise revenue for financing government services regarded as necessary, and whether registration facilitates the collection of taxes. It may do so either because a tax is imposed on the person who registers, or because the person who registers is used as a tax collector. For example, in collecting a sales tax imposed on various items of consumption, it is necessary to have a register or list of all the places selling goods subject to the tax.

Third, and this is the one possible justification for registration which is close to our main interest, registration may be a means to protect consumers against fraud. In general, liberal principles assign to the state the power to enforce contracts, and fraud involves the violation of a contract. It is, of course, dubious that one should go very far to protect in advance against fraud because of the interference with voluntary contracts involved in doing so. But I do not think that one can rule out on grounds of principle the possibility that there may be certain activities that are so likely to give rise to fraud as to render it desirable to have in advance a list of people known to be pursuing this activity. Perhaps one example along these lines is the registration of taxicab drivers. A taxicab driver picking up a person at night may be in a particularly good position to steal from him. To inhibit such practices, it may be desirable to have a list of names of people who are engaged in the taxicab business, to give each a number, and to require that this number be put in the cab so that anyone molested need only remember the number of the cab. This involves simply the use of the police power to protect individuals against violence on the part of other individuals and may be the most convenient method of doing so.

Certification is much more difficult to justify. The reason is that this is something the private market generally can do for itself. This problem is the same for products as for people's services. There are private certification agencies in many areas that certify the competence of a person or the quality of a particular product. The *Good Housekeeping* seal is a private certification arrangement. For industrial products there are private testing laboratories that will certify to the quality of a particular product. For consumer products, there are consumer testing agencies of which Consumer's Union and Consumer's Research are the best known in the United States. Better Business Bureaus are voluntary organizations that certify the quality of particular dealers. Technical schools, colleges, and universities certify the quality of their graduates. One function of retailers and department stores is to certify the quality of the many items they sell. The consumer develops confidence in the store, and the store in turn has an incentive to earn this confidence by investigating the quality of the items it sells.

One can however argue that in some cases, or perhaps even in many, voluntary certification will not be carried as far as individuals would be willing to pay for carrying it because of the difficulty of keeping the certification confidential. The issue is essentially the one involved in patents and copyrights, namely, whether individuals are in a position to capture the value of the services that they render to others. If I go into the business of certifying people, there may be no efficient way in which I can require you to pay for my certification. If I sell my certification information to one person, how can I keep him from passing it on to others? Consequently, it may not be possible to get effective voluntary exchange with respect to certification, even though this is a service that people would be willing to pay for if they had to. One way to get around this problem, as we get around other kinds of neighborhood effects, is to have governmental certification.

Another possible justification for certification is on monopoly grounds. There are some technical monopoly aspects to certification, since the cost of making a certification is largely independent of the number of people to whom the information is transmitted. However, it is by no means clear that monopoly is inevitable.

Licensure seems to me still more difficult to justify. It goes still farther in the direction of trenching upon the rights of individuals to enter into voluntary contracts. Nonetheless, there are some justifications given for licensure that the liberal will have to recognize as within his own conception of appropriate government action, though, as always, the advantages have to be weighed against the disadvantages. The main argument that is relevant to a liberal is the existence of neighborhood effects. The simplest and most obvious example is the "incompetent" physician who produces an epidemic. Insofar as he harms only his patient, that is simply a question of voluntary contract and exchange between the patient and his physician. On this score, there is no ground for intervention. However, it can be argued that if the physician treats his patient badly, he may unleash an epidemic that will cause harm to third parties who are not involved in the immediate transaction. In such a case, it is conceivable that everybody, including even the potential patient and physician, would be willing to submit to the restriction of the practice of medicine to "competent" people in order to prevent such epidemics from occurring.

In practice, the major argument given for licensure by its proponents is not this one, which has some appeal to a liberal, but rather a strictly paternalistic argument that has little or no appeal. Individuals, it is said, are incapable of choosing their own servants adequately, their own physician or plumber or barber. In order for a man to choose a physician intelligently, he would have to be a physician himself. Most of us, it is said, are therefore incompetent and we must be protected against our own ignorance. This amounts to saying that we in our capacity as voters must protect ourselves in our capacity as consumers against our own ignorance, by seeing to it that people are not served by incompetent physicians or plumbers or barbers.

So far, I have been listing the arguments for registration, certification, and licensing. In all three cases, it is clear that there are also strong social costs to be set against any of these advantages. Some of these social costs have already been suggested and I shall illustrate them in more detail for medicine, but it may be worth recording them here in general form.

The most obvious social cost is that any one of these measures, whether it be registration, certification, or licensure, almost inevitably becomes a tool in the hands of a special producer group to obtain a monopoly position at the expense of the rest of the public. There is no way to avoid this result. One can devise one or another set of procedural controls designed to avert this outcome, but none is likely to overcome the problem that arises out of the greater concentration of producer than of consumer interest. The people who are most concerned with any such arrangement, who will press most for its enforcement and be most concerned with its administration, will be the people in the particular occupation or trade involved. They will inevitably press for the extension of registration to certification and of certification to licensure. Once licensure is attained, the people who might develop an interest in undermining the regulations are kept from exerting their influence. They don't get a license, must therefore go into other occupations, and will lose interest. The result is invariably control over entry by members of the occupation itself and hence the establishment of a monopoly position.

Certification is much less harmful in this respect. If the certified "abuse" their special certificates; if, in certifying newcomers, members of the trade impose unnecessarily stringent requirements and reduce the number of practitioners too much, the price differential between certified and non-certified will become sufficiently large to induce the public to use non-certified practitioners. In technical terms, the elasticity of demand for the services of certified practitioners will be fairly large, and the limits within which they can exploit the rest of the public by taking advantage of their special position will be rather narrow.

In consequence, certification without licensure is a half-way house that maintains a good deal of protection against monopolization. It also has its disadvantages, but it is worth noting that the usual arguments for licensure, and in particular the paternalistic arguments, are satisfied almost entirely by certification alone. If the argument is that we are too ignorant to judge good practitioners, all that is needed is to make the relevant information available. If, in full knowledge, we still want to go to someone who is not certified, that is our business; we cannot complain that we did not have the information. Since arguments for licensure made by people who are not members of the occupation can be satisfied so fully by certification, I personally find it difficult to see any case for which licensure rather than certification can be justified.

Even registration has significant social costs. It is an important first step in the direction of a system in which every individual has to carry an identity card, every individual has to inform authorities what he plans to do before he does it. Moreover, as already noted, registration tends to be the first step toward certification and licensure.

MEDICAL LICENSURE

The medical profession is one in which practice of the profession has for a long time been restricted to people with licenses. Offhand, the question, "Ought we to let incompetent physicians practice?" seems to admit of only a negative answer. But I want to urge that second thought may give pause.

In the first place, licensure is the key to the control that the medical profession can exercise over the number of physicians. To understand why this is so requires some discussion of the structure of the medical profession. The American Medical Association is perhaps the strongest trade union in the United States. The essence of the power of a trade union is its power to restrict the number who may engage in a particular occupation. This restriction may be exercised indirectly by being able to enforce a wage rate higher than would otherwise prevail. If such a wage rate can be enforced, it will reduce the number of people who can get jobs and thus indirectly the number of people pursuing the occupation. This technique of restriction has disadvantages. There is always a dissatisfied fringe of people who are trying to get into the occupation. A trade union is much better off if it can limit directly the number of people who enter the occupation — who ever try to get jobs in it. The disgruntled and dissatisfied are excluded at the outset, and the union does not have to worry about them.

The American Medical Association is in this position. It is a trade union that can limit the number of people who can enter. How can it do this? The essential control is at the stage of admission to medical school. The Council on Medical Education and Hospitals of the American Medical Association approves medical schools. In order for a medical school to get and stay on its list of approved schools it has to meet the standards of the Council. The power of the Council has been demonstrated at various times when there has been pressure to reduce numbers. For example, in the 1930's during the depression, the Council on Medical Education and Hospitals wrote a letter to the various medical schools saying the medical schools were admitting more students than could be given the proper kind of training. In the next year or two, every school reduced the number it was admitting, giving very strong presumptive evidence that the recommendation had some effect.

Why does the Council's approval matter so much? If it abuses its power, why don't unapproved medical schools arise? The answer is that in almost every state in the United States, a person must be licensed to practice medicine, and to get the license, he must be a graduate of an approved school. In almost every state, the list of approved schools is identical with the list of schools approved by the Council on Medical Education and Hospitals of the American Medical Association. That is why the licensure provision is the key to the effective control of admission. It has a dual effect. On the one hand, the members of the licensure commission are always physicians and hence have some control at the step at which men apply for a license. This control is more limited in effectiveness than control at the medical school level. In almost all professions requiring licensure, people may try to get admitted more than once. If a person tries long enough and in enough jurisdictions he is likely to get through sooner or later. Since he has already spent the money and time to get his training, he has a strong incentive to keep trying. Licensure provisions that come into operation only after a man is trained therefore affect entry largely by raising the costs of getting into the occupation, since it may take a longer time to get in and since there is always some uncertainty whether he will succeed. But this rise in cost is nothing like so effective in limiting entry as is preventing a man from getting started on his career. If he is eliminated at the stage of entering medical school, he never comes up as a candidate for examination; he can never be troublesome at that stage. The efficient way to get control over the number in a profession is therefore to get control of entry into professional schools.

Control over admission to medical school and later licensure enables the profession to limit entry in two ways. The obvious one is simply by turning down many applicants. The less obvious, but probably far more important one, is by establishing standards for admission and licensure that make entry so difficult as to discourage young people from ever trying to get admission. Though most state laws require only two years of college prior to medical school, nearly 100 per cent of the entrants have had four years of college. Similarly, medical training proper has been lengthened, particularly through more stringent internship arrangements.

As an aside, the lawyers have never been as successful as the physicians in getting control at the point of admission to professional school, though they are moving in that direction. The reason is amusing. Almost every school on the American Bar

Association's list of approved schools is a full time day school; almost no night schools are approved. Many state legislators, on the other hand, are graduates of night law schools. If they voted to restrict admission to the profession to graduates of approved schools, in effect they would be voting that they themselves were not qualified. Their reluctance to condemn their own competence has been the main factor that has tended to limit the extent to which law has been able to succeed in imitating medicine. I have not myself done any extensive work on requirements for admission to law for many years but I understand that this limitation is breaking dꞋwn. The greater affluence of students means that a much larꞋer fraction are going to full time law schools and this is changing the composition of the legislatures.

To return to medicine, it is the provision about graduation from approved schools that is the most important source of professional control over entry. The profession has used this control to limit numbers. To avoid misunderstanding let me emphasize that I am not saying that individual members of the medical profession, the leaders of the medical profession, or the people who are in charge of the Council on Medical Education and Hospitals deliberately go out of their way to limit entry in order to raise their own incomes. That is not the way it works. Even when such people explicitly comment on the desirability of limiting numbers to raise incomes they will always justify the policy on the grounds that if "too" many people are let in, this will lower their incomes so that they will be driven to resort to unethical practices in order to earn a "proper" income. The only way, they argue, in which ethical practices can be maintained is by keeping people at a standard of income which is adequate to the merits and needs of the medical profession. I must confess that this has always seemed to me objectionable on both ethical and factual grounds. It is extraordinary that leaders of medicine should proclaim publicly that they and their colleagues must be paid to be ethical. And if it were so, I doubt that the price would have any limit. There seems little correlation between poverty and honesty. One would rather expect the opposite; dishonesty may not always pay but surely it sometimes does.

Control of entry is explicitly rationalized along these lines only at times like the Great Depression when there is much unemployment and relatively low incomes. In ordinary times, the rationalization for restriction is different. It is that the members of the medical profession want to raise what they regard as the standards of "quality" of the profession. The defect in this rationalization is a common one, and one that is destructive of a proper understanding of the operation of an economic system, namely, the failure to distinguish between technical efficiency and economic efficiency.

A story about lawyers will perhaps illustrate the point. At a meeting of lawyers at which problems of admission were being discussed, a colleague of mine, arguing against restrictive admission standards, used an analogy from the automobile industry. Would it not, he said, be absurd if the automobile industry were to argue that no one should drive a low quality car and therefore that no automobile manufacturer should be permitted to produce a car that did not come up to the Cadillac standard. One member of the audience rose and approved the analogy, saying that, of course, the country cannot afford anything but Cadillac lawyers! This tends to be the professional attitude. The members look solely at technical standards of performance, and argue in effect that we must have only first-rate physicians even if this means that some people get no medical service — though of course they never put it that way. Nonetheless, the view that people should get only the "optimum" medical service always lead to a restrictive policy, a policy that keeps down the number of physicians. I would not, of course, want to argue that this is the only force at work, but only that this kind of consideration leads many well-meaning physicians to go along with policies that they would reject out-of-hand if they did not have this kind of comforting rationalization.

It is easy to demonstrate that quality is only a rationalization and not the underlying reason for restriction. The power of the Council on Medical Education and Hospitals of the American Medical Association has been used to limit numbers in ways that cannot possibly have any connection whatsoever with quality. The simplest example is their recommendation to various states that citizenship be made a requirement for the practice of medicine. I find it inconceivable to see how this is relevant to medical performance. A similar requirement that they have tried to impose on occasion is that examination for licensure must be taken in English. A dramatic piece of evidence on the power and potency of the Association as well as on the lack of relation to quality is proved by one figure that I have always found striking. After 1933, when Hitler came to power in Germany, there was a tremendous outflow of professional people from Germany, Austria and so on, including of course, physicians who wanted to practice in the United States. The number of physicians trained abroad who were admitted to practice in the United States in the five years after 1933 was the same as in the five years before. This was clearly not the result of the natural course of events. The threat of these additional physicians led to a stringent tightening of requirements for foreign physicians that imposed extreme costs upon them.

It is clear that licensure is the key to the medical profession's ability to restrict the number of physicians who practice medicine. It is also the key to its ability to restrict technological and organizational changes in the way medicine is conducted. The American Medical Association has been consistently against the practice of group medicine, and against prepaid medical plans. These methods of practice may have good features and bad features, but they are technological innovations that people ought to be free to try out if they wish. There is no basis for saying conclusively that the optimum technical method of organizing medical practice is practice by an independent physician. Maybe it is group practice, maybe it is by corporations. One ought to have a system under which all varieties can be tried.

The American Medical Association has resisted such attempts and has been able effectively to inhibit them. It has been able to do so because licensure has indirectly given it control of admission to practice in hospitals. The Council on Medical Education and Hospitals approves hospitals as well as medical schools. In order for a physician to get admission to practice in an "approved" hospital, he must generally be approved by his county medical association or by the hospital board. Why can't unapproved hospitals be set up? Because under present economic conditions, in order for a hospital to operate it must have a supply of interns. Under most state licensure laws, candidates must have some internship experience to be admitted to practice, and internship must be in an "approved" hospital. The list of "approved" hospitals is generally identical with that of the Council on Medical Education and Hospitals. Consequently, the licensure law gives the profession control over hospitals as well as over schools. This is the key to the AMA's largely successful opposition to various types of group practice. In a few cases, the groups have been able to survive. In the District of Columbia, they succeeded because they were able to bring suit against the American Medical Association under the federal Sherman antitrust laws, and won the suit. In a few other cases, they have succeeded for special reasons. There is, however, no doubt that the tendency toward group practice has been greatly retarded by the AMA's opposition.

It is interesting, and this is an aside, that the medical association is against only one type of group practice, namely, prepaid group practice. The economic reason seems to be that this eliminates the possibility of engaging in discriminatory pricing.[8]

It is clear that licensure has been at the core of the restriction of entry and that this involves a heavy social cost, both to the individuals who want to practice medicine but are prevented from doing so and to the public deprived of the medical care it wants to buy and is prevented from buying. Let me now ask the question: Does licensure have the good effects that it is said to have?

In the first place, does it really raise standards of competence? It is by no means clear that it does raise the standards of competence in the actual practice of the profession for several reasons. In the first place, whenever you establish a block to entry into any field, you establish an incentive to find ways of getting around it, and of course medicine is no exception. The rise of the professions of osteopathy and of chiropractic is not unrelated to the restriction of entry into medicine. On the contrary, each of these represented, to some extent, an attempt to find a

[8] See Reuben Kessel, "Price Discrimination in Medicine," *The Journal of Law and Economics*, Vol. I (October, 1958), 20–53.

way around restriction of entry. Each of these, in turn, is proceeding to get itself licensed, and to impose restrictions. The effect is to create different levels and kinds of practice, to distinguish between what is called medical practice and substitutes such as osteopathy, chiropractic, faith healing and so on. These alternatives may well be of lower quality than medical practice would have been without the restrictions on entry into medicine.

More generally, if the number of physicians is less than it otherwise would be, and if they are all fully occupied, as they generally are, this means that there is a smaller total of medical practice by trained physicians—fewer medical man-hours of practice, as it were. The alternative is untrained practice by somebody; it may and in part must be by people who have no professional qualifications at all. Moreover, the situation is much more extreme. If "medical practice" is to be limited to licensed practitioners, it is necessary to define what medical practice is, and featherbedding is not something that is restricted to the railroads. Under the interpretation of the statutes forbidding unauthorized practice of medicine, many things are restricted to licensed physicians that could perfectly well be done by technicians, and other skilled people who do not have a Cadillac medical training. I am not enough of a technician to list the examples at all fully. I only know that those who have looked into the question say that the tendency is to include in "medical practice" a wider and wider range of activities that could perfectly well be performed by technicians. Trained physicians devote a considerable part of their time to things that might well be done by others. The result is to reduce drastically the amount of medical care. The relevant average quality of medical care, if one can at all conceive of the concept, cannot be obtained by simply averaging the quality of care that is given; that would be like judging the effectiveness of a medical treatment by considering only the survivors; one must also allow for the fact that the restrictions reduce the amount of care. The result may well be that the average level of competence in a meaningful sense has been reduced by the restrictions.

Even these comments do not go far enough, because they consider the situation at a point in time and do not allow for changes over time. Advances in any science or field often result from the work of one out of a large number of crackpots and quacks and people who have no standing in the profession. In the medical profession, under present circumstances, it is very difficult to engage in research or experimentation unless you are a member of the profession. If you are a member of the profession and want to stay in good standing in the profession, you are seriously limited in the kind of experimentation you can do. A "faith healer" may be just a quack who is imposing himself on credulous patients, but maybe one in a thousand or in many thousands will produce an important improvement in medicine. There are many different routes to knowledge and learning and the effect of restricting the practice of what is called medicine and defining it as we tend to do to a particular group, who in the main have to conform to the prevailing orthodoxy, is certain to reduce the amount of experimentation that goes on and hence to reduce the rate of growth of knowledge in the area. What is true for the content of medicine is true also for its organization, as has already been suggested. I shall expand further on this point below.

There is still another way in which licensure, and the associated monopoly in the practice of medicine, tend to render standards of practice low. I have already suggested that it renders the average quality of practice low by reducing the number of physicians, by reducing the aggregate number of hours available from trained physicians for more rather than less important tasks, and by reducing the incentive for research and development. It renders it low also by making it much more difficult for private individuals to collect from physicians for malpractice. One of the protections of the individual citizen against incompetence is protection against fraud and the ability to bring suit in the court against malpractice. Some suits are brought, and physicians complain a great deal about how much they have to pay for malpractice insurance. Yet suits for malpractice are fewer and less successful than they would be were it not for the watchful eye of the medical associations. It is not easy to get a physician to testify against a fellow physician when he faces the sanction of being denied the right to practice in an "approved" hospital. The testimony generally has to come from members of panels set up by medical associations themselves, always, of course, in the alleged interest of the patients.

When these effects are taken into account, I am myself persuaded that licensure has reduced both the quantity and quality of medical practice; that it has reduced the opportunities available to people who would like to be physicians, forcing them to pursue occupations they regard as less attractive; that it has forced the public to pay more for less satisfactory medical service, and that it has retarded technological development both in medicine itself and in the organization of medical practice. I conclude that licensure should be eliminated as a requirement for the practice of medicine.

When all this is said, many a reader, I suspect, like many a person with whom I have discussed these issues, will say, "But still, how else would I get any evidence on the quality of a physician. Granted all that you say about costs, is not licensure the only way of providing the public with some assurance of at least minimum quality ?" The answer is partly that people do not now choose physicians by picking names at random from a list of licensed physicians ; partly, that a man's ability to pass an examination twenty or thirty years earlier is hardly assurance of quality now ; hence, licensure is not now the main or even a major source of assurance of at least minimum quality. But the major answer is very different. It is that the question itself reveals the tyranny of the status quo and the poverty of our imagination in fields in which we are laymen, and even in those in which we have some competence, by comparison with the fertility of the market. Let me illustrate by speculating on how medicine might have developed and what assurances of quality would have emerged, if the profession had not exerted monopoly power.

Suppose that anyone had been free to practice medicine without restriction except for legal and financial responsibility for any harm done to others through fraud and negligence. I conjecture that the whole development of medicine would have been different. The present market for medical care, hampered as it has been, gives some hints of what the difference would have been. Group practice in conjunction with hospitals would have grown enormously. Instead of individual practice plus large institutional hospitals conducted by governments or eleemosynary institutions, there might have developed medical partnerships or corporations — medical teams. These would have provided central diagnostic and treatment facilities, including hospital facilities. Some presumably would have been prepaid, combining in one package present hospital insurance, health insurance, and group medical practice. Others would have charged separate fees for separate services. And of course, most might have used both methods of payment.

These medical teams — department stores of medicine, if you will — would be intermediaries between the patients and the physician. Being long-lived and immobile, they would have a great interest in establishing a reputation for reliability and quality. For the same reason, consumers would get to know their reputation. They would have the specialized skill to judge the quality of physicians; indeed, they would be the agent of the consumer in doing so, as the department store is now for many a product. In addition, they could organize medical care efficiently, combining medical men of different degrees of skill and training, using technicians with limited training for tasks for which they were suited, and reserving highly skilled and competent specialists for the tasks they alone could perform. The reader can add further flourishes for himself, drawing in part, as I have done, on what now goes on at the leading medical clinics.

Of course, not all medical practice would be done through such teams. Individual private practice would continue, just as the small store with a limited clientele exists alongside the department store, the individual lawyer alongside the great many-partnered firm. Men would establish individual reputations and some patients would prefer the privacy and intimacy of the individual practitioner. Some areas would be too small to be served by medical teams. And so on.

I would not even want to maintain that the medical teams would dominate the field. My aim is only to show by example that there are many alternatives to the present organization of practice. The impossibility of any individual or small group conceiving of all the possibilities, let alone evaluating their merits, is the great argument against central governmental planning and against arrangements such as professional monopolies that limit the possibilities of experimentation. On the other side, the great argument for the market is its tolerance of diversity; its ability to utilize a wide range of special knowledge and capacity. It renders special groups impotent to prevent experimentation and permits the customers and not the producers to decide what will serve the customers best.

Chapter X

The Distribution
of Income

A CENTRAL ELEMENT IN the development of a collectivist sentiment in this century, at least in Western countries, has been a
belief in equality of income as a social goal and a willingness to
use the arm of the state to promote it. Two very different questions must be asked in evaluating this egalitarian sentiment and
the egalitarian measures it has produced. The first is norma-
tive and ethical: what is the justification for state intervention to
promote equality? The second is positive and scientific: what
has been the effect of the measures actually taken?

THE ETHICS OF DISTRIBUTION

The ethical principle that would directly justify the distribution of income in a free market society is, "To each according to

what he and the instruments he owns produces." The operation
of even this principle implicitly depends on state action. Property rights are matters of law and social convention. As we have
seen, their definition and enforcement is one of the primary
functions of the state. The final distribution of income and
wealth under the full operation of this principle may well depend markedly on the rules of property adopted.

What is the relation between this principle and another that
seems ethically appealing, namely, equality of treatment? In
part, the two principles are not contradictory. Payment in accordance with product may be necessary to achieve true equality
of treatment. Given individuals whom we are prepared to regard as alike in ability and initial resources, if some have a
greater taste for leisure and others for marketable goods, inequality of return through the market is necessary to achieve
equality of total return or equality of treatment. One man may
prefer a routine job with much time off for basking in the sun
to a more exacting job paying a higher salary; another man may
prefer the opposite. If both were paid equally in money, their
incomes in a more fundamental sense would be unequal. Similarly, equal treatment requires that an individual be paid more
for a dirty, unattractive job than for a pleasant rewarding one.
Much observed inequality is of this kind. Differences of money
income offset differences in other characteristics of the occupation or trade. In the jargon of economists, they are "equalizing
differences" required to make the whole of the "net advantages," pecuniary and non-pecuniary, the same.

Another kind of inequality arising through the operation of
the market is also required, in a somewhat more subtle sense, to
produce equality of treatment, or to put it differently to satisfy
men's tastes. It can be illustrated most simply by a lottery. Consider a group of individuals who initially have equal endowments and who all agree voluntarily to enter a lottery with very
unequal prizes. The resultant inequality of income is surely required to permit the individuals in question to make the most
of their initial equality. Redistribution of the income after the
event is equivalent to denying them the opportunity to enter the
lottery. This case is far more important in practice than would
appear by taking the notion of a "lottery" literally. Individuals

choose occupations, investments, and the like partly in accordance with their taste for uncertainty. The girl who tries to become a movie actress rather than a civil servant is deliberately choosing to enter a lottery, so is the individual who invests in penny uranium stocks rather than government bonds. Insurance is a way of expressing a taste for certainty. Even these examples do not indicate fully the extent to which actual inequality may be the result of arrangements designed to satisfy men's tastes. The very arrangements for paying and hiring people are affected by such preferences. If all potential movie actresses had a great dislike of uncertainty, there would tend to develop "cooperatives" of movie actresses, the members of which agreed in advance to share income receipts more or less evenly, thereby in effect providing themselves insurance through the pooling of risks. If such a preference were widespread, large diversified corporations combining risky and non-risky ventures would become the rule. The wild-cat oil prospector, the private proprietorship, the small partnership, would all become rare.

Indeed, this is one way to interpret governmental measures to redistribute income through progressive taxes and the like. It can be argued that for one reason or another, costs of administration perhaps, the market cannot produce the range of lotteries or the kind of lottery desired by the members of the community, and that progressive taxation is, as it were, a government enterprise to do so. I have no doubt that this view contains an element of truth. At the same time, it can hardly justify present taxation, if only because the taxes are imposed *after* it is already largely known who have drawn the prizes and who the blanks in the lottery of life, and the taxes are voted mostly by those who think they have drawn the blanks. One might, along these lines, justify one generation's voting the tax schedules to be applied to an as yet unborn generation. Any such procedure would, I conjecture, yield income tax schedules much less highly graduated than present schedules are, at least on paper.

Though much of the inequality of income produced by payment in accordance with product reflects "equalizing" differences or the satisfaction of men's tastes for uncertainty, a large part reflects initial differences in endowment, both of human capacities and of property. This is the part that raises the really difficult ethical issue.

It is widely argued that it is essential to distinguish between inequality in personal endowments and in property, and between inequalities arising from inherited wealth and from acquired wealth. Inequality resulting from differences in personal capacities, or from differences in wealth accumulated by the individual in question, are considered appropriate, or at least not so clearly inappropriate as differences resulting from inherited wealth.

This distinction is untenable. Is there any greater ethical justification for the high returns to the individual who inherits from his parents a peculiar voice for which there is a great demand than for the high returns to the individual who inherits property? The sons of Russian commissars surely have a higher expectation of income — perhaps also of liquidation — than the sons of peasants. Is this any more or less justifiable than the higher income expectation of the son of an American millionaire? We can look at this same question in another way. A parent who has wealth that he wishes to pass on to his child can do so in different ways. He can use a given sum of money to finance his child's training as, say, a certified public accountant, or to set him up in business, or to set up a trust fund yielding him a property income. In any of these cases, the child will have a higher income than he otherwise would. But in the first case, his income will be regarded as coming from human capacities; in the second, from profits; in the third, from inherited wealth. Is there any basis for distinguishing among these categories of receipts on ethical grounds? Finally, it seems illogical to say that a man is entitled to what he has produced by personal capacities or to the produce of the wealth he has accumulated, but that he is not entitled to pass any wealth on to his children; to say that a man may use his income for riotous living but may not give it to his heirs. Surely, the latter is one way to use what he has produced.

The fact that these arguments against the so-called capitalist ethic are invalid does not of course demonstrate that the capitalist ethic is an acceptable one. I find it difficult to justify either accepting or rejecting it, or to justify any alternative principle.

I am led to the view that it cannot in and of itself be regarded as an ethical principle; that it must be regarded as instrumental or a corollary of some other principle such as freedom.

Some hypothetical examples may illustrate the fundamental difficulty. Suppose there are four Robinson Crusoes, independently marooned on four islands in the same neighborhood. One happened to land on a large and fruitful island which enables him to live easily and well. The others happened to land on tiny and rather barren islands from which they can barely scratch a living. One day, they discover the existence of one another. Of course, it would be generous of the Crusoe on the large island if he invited the others to join him and share its wealth. But suppose he does not. Would the other three be justified in joining forces and compelling him to share his wealth with them? Many a reader will be tempted to say yes. But before yielding to this temptation, consider precisely the same situation in different guise. Suppose you and three friends are walking along the street and you happen to spy and retrieve a $20 bill on the pavement. It would be generous of you, of course, if you were to divide it equally with them, or at least blow them to a drink. But suppose you do not. Would the other three be justified in joining forces and compelling you to share the $20 equally with them? I suspect most readers will be tempted to say no. And on further reflection, they may even conclude that the generous course of action is not itself clearly the "right" one. Are we prepared to urge on ourselves or our fellows that any person whose wealth exceeds the average of all persons in the world should immediately dispose of the excess by distributing it equally to all the rest of the world's inhabitants? We may admire and praise such action when undertaken by a few. But a universal "potlatch" would make a civilized world impossible.

In any event, two wrongs do not make a right. The unwillingness of the rich Robinson Crusoe or the lucky finder of the $20 bill to share his wealth does not justify the use of coercion by the others. Can we justify being judges in our own case, deciding on our own when we are entitled to use force to extract what we regard as our due from others? Or what we regard as not their due? Most differences of status or position or wealth can be regarded as the product of chance at a far enough remove. The man who is hard working and thrifty is to be regarded as "deserving"; yet these qualities owe much to the genes he was fortunate (or unfortunate?) enough to inherit.

Despite the lip service that we all pay to "merit" as compared to "chance," we are generally much readier to accept inequalities arising from chance than those clearly attributable to merit. The college professor whose colleague wins a sweepstake will envy him but is unlikely to bear him any malice or to feel unjustly treated. Let the colleague receive a trivial raise that makes his salary higher than the professor's own, and the professor is far more likely to feel aggrieved. After all, the goddess of chance, as of justice, is blind. The salary raise was a deliberate judgment of relative merit.

THE INSTRUMENTAL ROLE OF
DISTRIBUTION ACCORDING TO PRODUCT

The operative function of payment in accordance with product in a market society is not primarily distributive, but allocative. As was pointed out in chapter i, the central principle of a market economy is co-operation through voluntary exchange. Individuals co-operate with others because they can in this way satisfy their own wants more effectively. But unless an individual receives the whole of what he adds to the product, he will enter into exchanges on the basis of what he can receive rather than what he can produce. Exchanges will not take place that would have been mutually beneficial if each party received what he contributed to the aggregate product. Payment in accordance with product is therefore necessary in order that resources be used most effectively, at least under a system depending on voluntary co-operation. Given sufficient knowledge, it might be that compulsion could be substituted for the incentive of reward, though I doubt that it could. One can shuffle inanimate objects around; one can compel individuals to be at certain places at certain times; but one can hardly compel individuals to put forward their best efforts. Put another way, the substitution of compulsion for co-operation changes the amount of resources available.

Though the essential function of payment in accordance with product in a market society is to enable resources to be allocated efficiently without compulsion, it is unlikely to be tolerated unless it is also regarded as yielding distributive justice. No society can be stable unless there is a basic core of value judgments that are unthinkingly accepted by the great bulk of its members. Some key institutions must be accepted as "absolutes," not simply as instrumental. I believe that payment in accordance with product has been, and, in large measure, still is, one of these accepted value judgments or institutions.

One can demonstrate this by examining the grounds on which the internal opponents of the capitalist system have attacked the distribution of income resulting from it. It is a distinguishing feature of the core of central values of a society that it is accepted alike by its members, whether they regard themselves as proponents or as opponents of the system of organization of the society. Even the severest internal critics of capitalism have implicitly accepted payment in accordance with product as ethically fair.

The most far-reaching criticism has come from the Marxists. Marx argued that labor was exploited. Why? Because labor produced the whole of the product but got only part of it; the rest is Marx's "surplus value." Even if the statements of fact implicit in this assertion were accepted, the value judgment follows only if one accepts the capitalist ethic. Labor is "exploited" only if labor is entitled to what it produces. If one accepts instead the socialist premise, "to each according to his need, from each according to his ability" — whatever that may mean — it is necessary to compare what labor produces, not with what it gets but with its "ability", and to compare what labor gets, not with what it produces but with its "need."

Of course, the Marxist argument is invalid on other grounds as well. There is, first, the confusion between the total product of all co-operating resources and the amount added to product — in the economist's jargon, marginal product. Even more striking, there is an unstated change in the meaning of "labor" in passing from the premise to the conclusion. Marx recognized the role of capital in producing the product but regarded capital as embodied labor. Hence, written out in full, the premises of the Marxist syllogism would run: "Present and past labor produce the whole of the product. Present labor gets only part of the product." The logical conclusion is presumably "Past labor is exploited," and the inference for action is that past labor should get more of the product, though it is by no means clear how, unless it be in elegant tombstones.

The achievement of allocation of resources without compulsion is the major instrumental role in the market place of distribution in accordance with product. But it is not the only instrumental role of the resulting inequality. We have noted in chapter i the role that inequality plays in providing independent foci of power to offset the centralization of political power, as well as the role that it plays in promoting civil freedom by providing "patrons" to finance the dissemination of unpopular or simply novel ideas. In addition, in the economic sphere, it provides "patrons" to finance experimentation and the development of new products — to buy the first experimental automobiles and television sets, let alone impressionist paintings. Finally, it enables distribution to occur impersonally without the need for "authority" — a special facet of the general role of the market in effecting co-operation and co-ordination without coercion.

FACTS OF INCOME DISTRIBUTION

A capitalist system involving payment in accordance with product can be, and in practice is, characterized by considerable inequality of income and wealth. This fact is frequently misinterpreted to mean that capitalism and free enterprise produce wider inequality than alternative systems and, as a corollary, that the extension and development of capitalism has meant increased inequality. This misinterpretation is fostered by the misleading character of most published figures on the distribution of income, in particular their failure to distinguish short-run from long-run inequality. Let us look at some of the broader facts about the distribution of income.

One of the most striking facts which runs counter to many people's expectation has to do with the sources of income. The more capitalistic a country is, the smaller the fraction of income paid for the use of what is generally regarded as capital, and the larger the fraction paid for human services. In underdeveloped countries like India, Egypt, and so on, something like half of total income is property income. In the United States, roughly one-fifth is property income. And in other advanced capitalist countries, the proportion is not very different. Of course, these countries have much more capital than the primitive countries but they are even richer in the productive capacity of their residents; hence, the larger income from property is a smaller fraction of the total. The great achievement of capitalism has not been the accumulation of property, it has been the opportunities it has offered to men and women to extend and develop and improve their capacities. Yet the enemies of capitalism are fond of castigating it as materialist, and its friends all too often apologize for capitalism's materialism as a necessary cost of progress.

Another striking fact, contrary to popular conception, is that capitalism leads to less inequality than alternative systems of organization and that the development of capitalism has greatly lessened the extent of inequality. Comparisons over space and time alike confirm this view. There is surely drastically less inequality in Western capitalist societies like the Scandinavian countries, France, Britain, and the United States, than in a status society like India or a backward country like Egypt. Comparison with communist countries like Russia is more difficult because of paucity and unreliability of evidence. But if inequality is measured by differences in levels of living between the privileged and other classes, such inequality may well be decidedly less in capitalist than in communist countries. Among the Western countries alone, inequality appears to be less, in any meaningful sense, the more highly capitalist the country is: less in Britain than in France, less in the United States than in Britain — though these comparisons are rendered difficult by the problem of allowing for the intrinsic heterogeneity of populations; for a fair comparison, for example, one should perhaps compare the United States, not with the United Kingdom alone but with the United Kingdom plus the West Indies plus its African possessions.

With respect to changes over time, the economic progress achieved in the capitalist societies has been accompanied by a drastic diminution in inequality. As late as 1848, John Stuart Mill could write, "Hitherto [1848] it is questionable if all the mechanical inventions yet made have lightened the day's toil of any human being. They have enabled a greater population to live the same life of drudgery and imprisonment, and an increased number of manufacturers and others to make fortunes. They have increased the comforts of the middle classes. But they have not yet begun to effect those great changes in human destiny, which it is in their nature and in their futurity to accomplish."[1] This statement was probably not correct even for Mill's day, but certainly no one could write this today about the advanced capitalist countries. It is still true about the rest of the world.

The chief characteristic of progress and development over the past century is that it has freed the masses from backbreaking toil and has made available to them products and services that were formerly the monopoly of the upper classes, without in any corresponding way expanding the products and services available to the wealthy. Medicine aside, the advances in technology have for the most part simply made available to the masses of the people luxuries that were always available in one form or another to the truly wealthy. Modern plumbing, central heating, automobiles, television, radio, to cite just a few examples, provide conveniences to the masses equivalent to those that the wealthy could always get by the use of servants, entertainers, and so on.

Detailed statistical evidence on these phenomena, in the form of meaningful and comparable distributions of income, is hard to come by, though such studies as have been made confirm the broad conclusions just outlined. Such statistical data, however, can be extremely misleading. They cannot segregate differences in income that are equalizing from those that are not. For example, the short working life of a baseball player means that the annual income during his active years must be much higher than in alternative pursuits open to him to make it equally attractive financially. But such a difference affects the figures in exactly the same way as any other difference in in-

[1] *Principles of Political Economy* (Ashley edition; London: Longmans, Green & Co., 1909), p. 751.

come. The income unit for which the figures are given is also of great importance. A distribution for individual income recipients always shows very much greater apparent inequality than a distribution for family units: many of the individuals are housewives working part-time or receiving a small amount of property income, or other family members in a similar position. Is the distribution that is relevant for families one in which the families are classified by total family income? Or by income per person? Or per equivalent unit? This is no mere quibble. I believe that the changing distribution of families by number of children is the most important single factor that has reduced inequality of levels of living in this country during the past half century. It has been far more important than graduated inheritance and income taxes. The really low levels of living were the joint product of relatively low family incomes and relatively large numbers of children. The average number of children has declined and, even more important, this decline has been accompanied and largely produced by a virtual elimination of the very large family. As a result, families now tend to differ much less with respect to number of children. Yet this change would not be reflected in a distribution of families by the size of total family income.

A major problem in interpreting evidence on the distribution of income is the need to distinguish two basically different kinds of inequality; temporary, short-run differences in income, and differences in long-run income status. Consider two societies that have the same distribution of annual income. In one there is great mobility and change so that the position of particular families in the income hierarchy varies widely from year to year. In the other, there is great rigidity so that each family stays in the same position year after year. Clearly, in any meaningful sense, the second would be the more unequal society. The one kind of inequality is a sign of dynamic change, social mobility, equality of opportunity; the other, of a status society. The confusion of these two kinds of inequality is particularly important, precisely because competitive free-enterprise capitalism tends to substitute the one for the other. Non-capitalist societies tend to have wider inequality than capitalist, even as measured by annual income; in addition, inequality in them tends to be permanent, whereas capitalism undermines status and introduces social mobility.

The methods that governments have used most widely to alter the distribution of income have been graduated income and inheritance taxation. Before considering their desirability, it is worth asking whether they have succeeded in their aim.

No conclusive answer can be given to this question with our present knowledge. The judgment that follows is a personal, though I hope not utterly uninformed, opinion, stated, for sake of brevity, more dogmatically than the nature of the evidence justifies. My impression is that these tax measures have had a relatively minor, though not negligible, effect in the direction of narrowing the differences between the average position of groups of families classified by some statistical measures of income. However, they have also introduced essentially arbitrary inequalities of comparable magnitude between persons within such income classes. As a result, it is by no means clear whether the net effect in terms of the basic objective of equality of treatment or equality of outcome has been to increase or decrease equality.

The tax rates are on paper both high and highly graduated. But their effect has been dissipated in two different ways. First, part of their effect has been simply to make the pre-tax distribution more unequal. This is the usual incidence effect of taxation. By discouraging entry into activities highly taxed — in this case activities with large risk and non-pecuniary disadvantages — they raise returns in those activities. Second, they have stimulated both legislative and other provisions to evade the tax — so-called "loopholes" in the law such as percentage depletion, exemption of interest on state and municipal bonds, specially favorable treatment of capital gains, expense accounts, other indirect ways of payment, conversion of ordinary income to capital gains, and so on in bewildering number and kind. The effect has been to make the actual rates imposed far lower than the nominal rates and, perhaps more important, to make the incidence of the taxes capricious and unequal. People at the same economic level pay very different taxes depending on the accident of the source of their income and the opportunities they have to evade the tax. If present rates were made fully effective, the effect on incentives and the like might well be so serious as to cause a radical loss in the productivity of the society. Tax avoidance may therefore have been essential for economic well-being. If so, the gain has been bought at the cost of a great waste of resources, and of the introduction of widespread inequity. A much lower set of nominal rates, plus a more comprehensive base through more equal taxation of all sources of income could be both more progressive in average incidence, more equitable in detail, and less wasteful of resources.

This judgment that the personal income tax has been arbitrary in its impact and of limited effectiveness in reducing inequality is widely shared by students of the subject, including many who strongly favor the use of graduated taxation to reduce inequality. They too urge that the top bracket rates be drastically reduced and the base broadened.

A further factor that has reduced the impact of the graduated tax structure on inequality of income and wealth is that these taxes are much less taxes on being wealthy than on becoming wealthy. While they limit the use of the income from existing wealth, they impede even more strikingly — so far as they are effective — the accumulation of wealth. The taxation of the income from the wealth does nothing to reduce the wealth itself, it simply reduces the level of consumption and additions to wealth that the owners can support. The tax measures give an incentive to avoid risk and to embody existing wealth in relatively stable forms, which reduces the likelihood that existing accumulations of wealth will be dissipated. On the other side, the major route to new accumulations is through large current incomes of which a large fraction is saved and invested in risky activities, some of which will yield high returns. If the income tax were effective, it would close this route. In consequence, its effect would be to protect existing holders of wealth from the competition of newcomers. In practice, this effect is largely dissipated by the avoidance devices already referred to. It is notable how large a fraction of the new accumuations have been in oil, where the percentage depletion allowances provide a particularly easy route to the receipt of tax-free income.

In judging the desirability of graduated income taxation it seems to me important to distinguish two problems, even though the distinction cannot be precise in application: first, the raising of funds to finance the expenses of those governmental activities it is decided to undertake (including perhaps measures to eliminate poverty discussed in chapter xii); second, the imposition of taxes for redistributive purposes alone. The former might well call for some measure of graduation, both on grounds of assessing costs in accordance with benefits and on grounds of social standards of equity. But the present high nominal rates on top brackets of income and inheritance can hardly be justified on this ground — if only because their yield is so low.

I find it hard, as a liberal, to see any justification for graduated taxation solely to redistribute income. This seems a clear case of using coercion to take from some in order to give to others and thus to conflict head-on with individual freedom.

All things considered, the personal income tax structure that seems to me best is a flat-rate tax on income above an exemption, with income defined very broadly and deductions allowed only for strictly defined expenses of earning income. As already suggested in chapter v, I would combine this program with the abolition of the corporate income tax, and with the requirement that corporations be required to attribute their income to stockholders, and that stockholders be required to include such sums on their tax returns. The most important other desirable changes are the elimination of percentage depletion on oil and other raw materials, the elimination of tax exemption of interest on state and local securities, the elimination of special treatment of capital gains, the co-ordination of income, estate, and gift taxes, and the elimination of numerous deductions now allowed.

An exemption, it seems to me, can be a justified degree of graduation (see further discussion in chapter xii). It is very different for 90 per cent of the population to vote taxes on themselves and an exemption for 10 per cent than for 90 per cent to vote punitive taxes on the other 10 per cent — which is in effect what has been done in the United States. A proportional flat-rate-tax would involve higher absolute payments by persons with higher incomes for governmental services, which is not clearly inappropriate on grounds of benefits conferred. Yet it would avoid a situation where any large numbers could vote to impose on others taxes that did not also affect their own tax burden.

The proposal to substitute a flat-rate income tax for the present graduated rate structure will strike many a reader as a radical proposal. And so it is in terms of concept. For this very reason, it cannot be too strongly emphasized that it is not radical in terms of revenue yield, redistribution of income, or any other relevant criterion. Our present income tax rates range from 20 per cent to 91 per cent, with the rate reaching 50 per cent on the excess of taxable incomes over $18,000 for single taxpayers or $36,000 for married taxpayers filing joint returns. Yet a flat rate of 23½ per cent on taxable income as presently reported and presently defined, that is, above present exemptions and after all presently allowable deductions, would yield as much revenue as the present highly graduated rate.[2] In fact, such a flat rate, even with no change whatsoever in other features of the law, would yield a higher revenue because a larger amount of taxable income would be reported for three reasons: there would be less incentive than now to adopt legal but costly schemes that reduce the amount of taxable income reported (so-called tax avoidance); there would be less incentive to fail to report income that legally should be reported (tax evasion); the removal of the disincentive effects of the present structure of rates would produce a more efficient use of present resources and a higher income.

If the yield of the present highly graduated rates is so low, so

[2] This point is so important that it may be worth giving the figures and calculations. The latest year for which figures are available as this is written is the taxable year 1959 in U. S. Internal Revenue Service, *Statistics of Income for 1959.* For that year: Aggregate taxable income reported on

Individual tax returns... $166,540 million
Income Tax before tax credit .... 39,092 million
Income tax after tax credit... 38,645 million

A flat rate tax of 23½ per cent on the aggregate taxable income would have yielded (.235) × $166,540 million = $39,137 million.

If we assume the same tax credit, the final yield would have been about the same as that actually attained.

also must be their redistributive effects. This does not mean that they do no harm. On the contrary. The yield is so low partly because some of the most competent men in the country devote their energies to devising ways to keep it so low; and because many other men shape their activities with one eye on tax effects. All this is sheer waste. And what do we get for it? At most, a feeling of satisfaction on the part of some that the state is redistributing income. And even this feeling is founded on ignorance of the actual effects of the graduated tax structure, and would surely evaporate if the facts were known.

To return to the distribution of income, there is a clear justification for social action of a very different kind than taxation to affect the distribution of income. Much of the actual inequality derives from imperfections of the market. Many of these have themselves been created by government action or could be removed by government action. There is every reason to adjust the rules of the game so as to eliminate these sources of inequality. For example, special monopoly privileges granted by government, tariffs, and other legal enactments benefiting particular groups, are a source of inequality. The removal of these, the liberal will welcome. The extension and widening of educational opportunities has been a major factor tending to reduce inequalities. Measures such as these have the operational virtue that they strike at the sources of inequality rather than simply alleviating the symptoms.

The distribution of income is still another area in which government has been doing more harm by one set of measures than it has been able to undo by others. It is another example of the justification of government intervention in terms of alleged defects of the private enterprise system when many of the phenomena of which champions of big government complain are themselves the creation of government, big and small.

Chapter XI

Social Welfare Measures

THE HUMANITARIAN AND EGALITARIAN sentiment which helped produce the steeply graduated individual income tax has also produced a host of other measures directed at promoting the "welfare" of particular groups. The most important single set of measures is the bundle misleadingly labeled "social security." Others are public housing, minimum wage laws, farm price supports, medical care for particular groups, special aid programs, and so on.

I shall first discuss briefly a few of the latter, mostly to indicate how different their actual effects may be from those intended, and shall then discuss at somewhat greater length the largest single component of the social security program, old age and survivor's insurance.

MISCELLANEOUS WELFARE MEASURES

1. *Public Housing*   One argument frequently made for public housing is based on an alleged neighborhood effect: slum districts in particular, and other low quality housing to a lesser degree, are said to impose higher costs on the community in the form of fire and police protection. This literal neighborhood effect may well exist. But insofar as it does, it alone argues, not for public housing, but for higher taxes on the kind of housing that adds to social costs since this would tend to equalize private and social cost.

It will be answered at once that the extra taxes would bear on low-income people and that this is undesirable. The answer means that public housing is proposed not on the ground of neighborhood effects but as a means of helping low-income people. If this be the case, why subsidize housing in particular? If funds are to be used to help the poor, would they not be used more effectively by being given in cash rather than in kind? Surely, the families being helped would rather have a given sum in cash than in the form of housing. They could themselves spend the money on housing if they so desired. Hence, they would never be worse off if given cash; if they regarded other needs as more important, they would be better off. The cash subsidy would solve the neighborhood effect as well as the subsidy in kind, since if it were not used to buy housing it would be available to pay extra taxes justified by the neighborhood effect.

Public housing cannot therefore be justified on the grounds either of neighborhood effects or of helping poor families. It can be justified, if at all, only on grounds of paternalism; that the families being helped "need" housing more than they "need" other things but would themselves either not agree or would spend the money unwisely. The liberal will be inclined to reject this argument for responsible adults. He cannot completely reject it in the more indirect form in which it affects children; namely, that parents will neglect the welfare of the children, who "need" the better housing. But he will surely demand evidence much more persuasive and to the point than the kind usually given before he can accept this final argument as adequate justification for large expenditures on public housing.

So much could have been said in the abstract, in advance of actual experience with public housing. Now that we have had experience, we can go much farther. In practice, public housing has turned out to have effects very different indeed from those intended.

Far from improving the housing of the poor, as its proponents expected, public housing has done just the reverse. The number of dwelling units destroyed in the course of erecting public housing projects has been far larger than the number of new dwelling units constructed. But public housing as such has done nothing to reduce the number of persons to be housed. The effect of public housing has therefore been to raise the number of persons per dwelling unit. Some families have probably been better housed than they would otherwise have been — those who were fortunate enough to get occupancy of the publicly built units. But this has only made the problem for the rest all the worse, since the average density of all together went up.

Of course, private enterprise offset some of the deleterious effect of the public housing program by conversion of existing quarters and construction of new ones for either the persons directly displaced or, more generally, the persons displaced at one or two removes in the game of musical chairs set in motion by the public housing projects. However, these private resources would have been available in the absence of the public housing program.

Why did the public housing program have this effect? For the general reason we have stressed time and again. The general interest that motivated many to favor instituting the program is diffuse and transitory. Once the program was adopted, it was bound to be dominated by the special interests that it could serve. In this case, the special interests were those local groups that were anxious to have blighted areas cleared and refurbished, either because they owned property there or because the blight was threatening local or central business districts. Public housing served as a convenient means to accomplish their objective, which required more destruction than construction.

Even so, "urban blight" is still with us in undiminished force, to judge by the growing pressure for federal funds to deal with it.

Another gain its proponents expected from public housing was the reduction of juvenile delinquency by improving housing conditions. Here again, the program in many instances had precisely the opposite effect, entirely aside from its failure to improve *average* housing conditions. The income limitations quite properly imposed for the occupancy of public housing at subsidized rentals have led to a very high density of "broken" families —in particular, divorced or widowed mothers with children. Children of broken families are especially likely to be "problem" children and a high concentration of such children is likely to increase juvenile delinquency. One manifestation has been the very adverse effect on schools in the neighborhood of a public housing project. Whereas a school can readily absorb a few "problem" children it is very difficult for it to absorb a large number. Yet in some cases, broken families are a third or more of the total in a public housing project and the project may account for a majority of the children in the school. Had these families been assisted through cash grants, they would have been spread much more thinly through the community.

2. *Minimum wage laws* Minimum wage laws are about as clear a case as one can find of a measure the effects of which are precisely the opposite of those intended by the men of good will who support it. Many proponents of minimum wage laws quite properly deplore extremely low rates; they regard them as a sign of poverty; and they hope, by outlawing wage rates below some specified level, to reduce poverty. In fact, insofar as minimum wage laws have any effect at all, their effect is clearly to increase poverty. The state can legislate a minimum wage rate. It can hardly require employers to hire at that minimum all who were formerly employed at wages below the minimum. It is clearly not in the interest of employers to do so. The effect of the minimum wage is therefore to make unemployment higher than it otherwise would be. Insofar as the low wage rates are in fact a sign of poverty, the people who are rendered unemployed are precisely those who can least afford

to give up the income they had been receiving, small as it may appear to the people voting for the minimum wage.

This case is in one respect very much like public housing. In both, the people who are helped are visible — the people whose wages are raised; the people who occupy the publicly built units. The people who are hurt are anonymous and their problem is not clearly connected to its cause: the people who join the ranks of the unemployed or, more likely, are never employed in particular activities because of the existence of the minimum wage and are driven to even less remunerative activities or to the relief rolls; the people who are pressed ever closer together in the spreading slums that seem to be rather a sign of the need for more public housing than a consequence of the existing public housing.

A large part of the support for minimum wage laws comes not from disinterested men of good will but from interested parties. For example, northern trade unions and northern firms threatened by southern competition favor minimum wage laws to reduce the competition from the South.

3. *Farm price supports* Farm price supports are another example. Insofar as they can be justified at all on grounds other than the political fact that rural areas are over-represented in the electoral college and Congress, it must be on the belief that farmers on the average have low incomes. Even if this be accepted as a fact, farm price supports do not accomplish the intended purpose of helping the farmers who need help. In the first place, benefits are, if anything, inverse to need, since they are in proportion to the amount sold on the market. The impecunious farmer not only sells less on the market than the wealthier farmer; in addition, he gets a larger fraction of his income from products grown for his own use, and these do not qualify for the benefits. In the second place, the benefits, if any, to farmers from the price-support program are much smaller than the total amount spent. This is clearly true of the amount spent for storage and similar costs which does not go to the farmer at all — indeed the suppliers of storage capacity and facilities may well be the major beneficiaries. It is equally true of the amount spent to purchase agricultural products. The

farmer is thereby induced to spend additional sums on ferti-
lizer, seed, machinery, etc. At most, only the excess adds to his
income. And finally, even this residual of a residual overstates
the gain since the effect of the program has been to keep more
people on the farm than would otherwise have stayed there.
Only the excess, if any, of what they can earn on the farm with
the price-support program over what they can earn off the
farm, is a net benefit to them. The main effect of the purchase
program has simply been to make farm output larger, not to
raise the income per farmer.

Some of the costs of the farm purchase program are so obvious and well-known as to need little more than mention: the
consumer has paid twice, once in taxes for farm benefit payments, again by paying a higher price for food; the farmer has
been saddled with onerous restrictions and detailed centralized
control; the nation has been saddled with a spreading bureaucracy. There is, however, one set of costs which is less well-
known. The farm program has been a major hindrance in the
pursuit of foreign policy. In order to maintain a higher domestic
than world price, it has been necessary to impose quotas on imports for many items. Erratic changes in our policy have had
serious adverse effects on other countries. A high price for cotton
encouraged other countries to enlarge their cotton production.
When our high price led to an unwieldy stock of cotton, we
proceeded to sell overseas at low prices and imposed heavy losses
on the producers whom we had by our earlier actions encouraged to expand output. The list of similar cases could be
multiplied.

OLD AGE AND SURVIVOR'S INSURANCE

The "social security" program is one of those things on which
the tyranny of the status quo is beginning to work its magic.
Despite the controversy that surrounded its inception, it has
come to be so much taken for granted that its desirability is
hardly questioned any longer. Yet it involves a large-scale in-
vasion into the personal lives of a large fraction of the nation
without, so far as I can see, any justification that is at all persuasive, not only on liberal principles, but on almost any other. I

propose to examine the biggest phase of it, that which involves payments to the aged.

As an operational matter, the program known as old age and survivor's insurance (OASI) consists of a special tax imposed on payrolls, plus payments to persons who have reached a specified age, of amounts determined by the age at which payments begin, family status, and prior earning record.

As an analytical matter, OASI consists of three separable elements:

1. The requirement that a wide class of persons must purchase specified annuities, i.e., compulsory provision for old age.

2. The requirement that the annuity must be purchased from the government; i.e., nationalization of the provision of these annuities.

3. A scheme for redistributing income, insofar as the value of the annuities to which people are entitled when they enter the system is not equal to the taxes they will pay.

Clearly, there is no necessity for these elements to be combined. Each individual could be required to pay for his own annuity; the individual could be permitted to purchase an annuity from private firms; yet individuals could be required to purchase specified annuities. The government could go into the business of selling annuities without compelling individuals to buy specified annuities and require the business to be self-supporting. And clearly the government can and does engage in redistribution without using the device of annuities.

Let us therefore consider each of these elements in turn to see how far, if at all, each can be justified. It will facilitate our analysis, I believe, if we consider them in reverse order.

1. Income redistribution. The present OASI program involves two major kinds of redistribution; from some OASI beneficiaries to others; from the general taxpayer to OASI beneficiaries.

The first kind of redistribution is primarily from those who entered the system relatively young, to those who entered it at an advanced age. The latter are receiving, and will for some time be receiving, a greater amount as benefits than the taxes they paid could have purchased. Under present tax and benefit schedules, on the other hand, those who entered the system at a young age will receive decidedly less.

I do not see any grounds — liberal or other — on which this particular redistribution can be defended. The subsidy to the beneficiaries is independent of their poverty or wealth; the man of means receives it as much as the indigent. The tax which pays the subsidy is a flat-rate tax on earnings up to a maximum. It constitutes a larger fraction of low incomes than of high. What conceivable justification is there for taxing the young to subsidize the old regardless of the economic status of the old; for imposing a higher rate of tax for this purpose on the low incomes than on the high; or, for that matter, for raising the revenues to pay the subsidy by a tax on payrolls?

The second kind of redistribution arises because the system is not likely to be fully self-financing. During the period when many were covered and paying taxes, and few had qualified for benefits, the system appeared to be self-financing and indeed to be having a surplus. But this appearance depends on neglecting the obligation being accumulated with respect to the persons paying the tax. It is doubtful that the taxes paid have sufficed to finance the accumulated obligation. Many experts assert that even on a cash basis, a subsidy will be required. And such a subsidy generally has been required in similar systems in other countries. This is a highly technical matter which we cannot and need not go into here and about which there can be honest differences of opinion.

For our purpose, it is enough to ask only the hypothetical question whether a subsidy from the general taxpayer could be justified if it is required. I see no grounds on which such a subsidy can be justified. We may wish to help poor people. Is there any justification for helping people whether they are poor or not because they happen to be a certain age? Is this not an entirely arbitrary redistribution?

The only argument I have ever come across to justify the redistribution involved in OASI is one that I regard as thoroughly immoral despite its wide use. This argument is that OASI redistribution on the average helps low-income people more than high-income people despite a large arbitrary element; that it would be better to do this redistribution more efficiently; but that the community will not vote for the redistribution directly though it will vote for it as part of a social security package. In essence, what this argument says is that the community can be fooled into voting for a measure that it opposes by presenting the measure in a false guise. Needless to say, the people who argue this way are the loudest in their condemnation of "misleading" commercial advertising![1]

2. *Nationalization of the provision of required annuities* Suppose we avoid redistribution by requiring each person to pay for the annuity he gets, in the sense of course, that the premium suffices to cover the present value of the annuity, account being taken both of mortality and interest returns. What justification is there then for requiring him to purchase it from a governmental concern? If redistribution is to be accomplished, clearly the taxing power of the government must be used. But if redistribution is to be no part of the program and, as we have just seen, it is hard to see any justification for making it part, why not permit individuals who wish to do so to purchase their annuities from private concerns? A close analogy is provided by state laws requiring compulsory purchase of automobile liability insurance. So far as I know, no state which has such a law even has a state insurance company, let alone compels automobile owners to buy their insurance from a government agency.

Possible economies of scale are no argument for nationalizing the provision of annuities. If they are present, and the government sets up a concern to sell annuity contracts, it may be able to undersell competitors by virtue of its size. In that case, it will get the business without compulsion. If it cannot undersell

[1] Another current example of the same argument is in connection with proposals for federal subsidies for schooling (misleadingly labeled, "aid to education"). A case can be made for using federal funds to supplement schooling expenditures in the states with the lowest incomes, on the grounds that the children schooled may migrate to other states. There is no case whatsoever for imposing taxes on all the states and giving federal subsidies to all the states. Yet every bill introduced into Congress provides for the latter and not the former. Some proponents of these bills, who recognize that only subsidies to some states can be justified, defend their position by saying that a bill providing only for such subsidies could not be passed and that the only way to get disproportionate subsidies to poorer states is to include them in a bill providing subsidies to all states.

them, then presumably economies of scale are not present or are not sufficient to overcome other diseconomies of governmental operation.

One possible advantage of nationalizing the provision of annuities is to facilitate the enforcement of compulsory purchase of annuities. However, this seems a rather trivial advantage. It would be easy to devise alternative administrative arrangements, such as requiring individuals to include a copy of a receipt for premium payments along with their income tax returns; or having their employers certify to their having met the requirement. The administrative problem would surely be minor compared with that imposed by the present arrangements.

The costs of nationalization seem clearly to outweigh any such trivial advantage. Here, as elsewhere, individual freedom to choose, and competition of private enterprises for custom, would promote improvements in the kinds of contracts available, and foster variety and diversity to meet individual need. On the political level, there is the obvious gain from avoiding an expansion in the scale of governmental activity and the indirect threat to freedom of every such expansion.

Some less obvious political costs arise from the character of the present program. The issues involved become very technical and complex. The layman is often incompetent to judge them. Nationalization means that the bulk of the "experts" become employees of the nationalized system, or university people closely linked with it. Inevitably, they come to favor its expansion, not, I hasten to add, out of narrow self-interest but because they are operating within a framework in which they take for granted governmental administration and are familiar only with its techniques. The only saving grace in the United States so far has been the existence of private insurance companies involved in similar activities.

Effective control by Congress over the operations of such agencies as the Social Security Administration becomes essentially impossible as a result of the technical character of their task and their near-monopoly of experts. They become self-governing bodies whose proposals are in the main rubber-stamped by Congress. The able and ambitious men who make their careers in them are naturally anxious to expand the scope of their agencies and it is exceedingly difficult to prevent them from doing so. If the expert says yea, who is there competent to say nay? So we have seen an increasing fraction of the population drawn into the social security system, and now that there remain few possibilities of expansion in that direction, we are seeing a move toward the addition of new programs, such as medical care.

I conclude that the case against the nationalization of the provision of annuities is exceedingly strong, not only in terms of liberal principles but even in terms of the values expressed by proponents of the welfare state. If they believe that the government can provide the service better than the market, they should favor a government concern to issue annuities in open competition with other concerns. If they are right, the government concern will prosper. If they are wrong, the welfare of the people will be advanced by having a private alternative. Only the doctrinaire socialist, or the believer in centralized control for its own sake, can, so far as I can see, take a stand on principle in favor of nationalization of the provision of annuities.

3. *Compulsory Purchase of Annuities* Having cleared away the underbrush, we are now ready to face the key issue: compelling individuals to use some of their current income to purchase annuities to provide for their old age.

One possible justification for such compulsion is strictly paternalistic. People could if they wished decide to do individually what the law requires them to do as a group. But they are separately short-sighted and improvident. "We" know better than "they" that it is in their own good to provide for their old age to a greater extent than they would voluntarily; we cannot persuade them individually; but we can persuade 51 per cent or more to compel all to do what is in their own good. This paternalism is for responsible people, hence does not even have the excuse of concern for children or madmen.

This position is internally consistent and logical. A thoroughgoing paternalist who holds it cannot be dissuaded by being shown that he is making a mistake in logic. He is our opponent on grounds of principle, not simply a well-meaning but misguided friend. Basically, he believes in dictatorship, benevolent and maybe majoritarian, but dictatorship none the less.

Those of us who believe in freedom must believe also in the freedom of individuals to make their own mistakes. If a man knowingly prefers to live for today, to use his resources for current enjoyment, deliberately choosing a penurious old age, by what right do we prevent him from doing so? We may argue with him, seek to persuade him that he is wrong, but are we entitled to use coercion to prevent him from doing what he chooses to do? Is there not always the possibility that he is right and that we are wrong? Humility is the distinguishing virtue of the believer in freedom; arrogance, of the paternalist.

Few people are thoroughgoing paternalists. It is a position that is most unattractive if examined in the cold light of the day. Yet the paternalistic argument has played so large a role in measures like social security that it seems worth making it explicit.

A possible justification on liberal principles for compulsory purchase of annuities is that the improvident will not suffer the consequence of their own action but will impose costs on others. We shall not, it is said, be willing to see the indigent aged suffer in dire poverty. We shall assist them by private and public charity. Hence the man who does not provide for his old age will become a public charge. Compelling him to buy an annuity is justified not for his own good but for the good of the rest of us.

The weight of this argument clearly depends on fact. If 90 per cent of the population would become charges on the public at age 65 in the absence of compulsory purchase of annuities, the argument would have great weight. If only 1 per cent would, the argument has none. Why restrict the freedom of 99 per cent to avoid the costs that the other 1 per cent would impose on the community?

The belief that a large fraction of the community would become public charges if not compelled to purchase annuities owed its plausibility, at the time OASI was enacted, to the Great Depression. In every year from 1931 through 1940, more than one-seventh of the labor force was unemployed. And unemployment was proportionately heavier among the older workers. This experience was unprecedented and has not been repeated since. It did not arise because people were improvident and failed to provide for their old age. It was a consequence, as we have seen, of government mismanagement. OASI is a cure, if cure it be at all, for a very different malady and one of which we have had no experience.

The unemployed of the 1930's certainly created a serious problem of the relief of distress, of many people becoming public charges. But old-age was by no means the most serious problem. Many people in productive ages were on the relief or assistance rolls. And the steady spread of OASI, until today more than sixteen million persons receive benefits, has not prevented a continued growth in the number receiving public assistance.

Private arrangements for the care of the aged have altered greatly over time. Children were at one time the major means whereby people provided for their own old age. As the community became more affluent, the mores changed. The responsibilities imposed on children to care for their parents declined and more and more people came to make provision for old age in the form of accumulating property or acquiring private pension rights. More recently, the development of pension plans over and above OASI has accelerated. Indeed, some students believe that a continuation of present trends points to a society in which a large fraction of the public scrimps in their productive years to provide themselves with a higher standard of life in old age than they ever enjoyed in the prime of life. Some of us may think such a trend perverse, but if it reflects the tastes of the community, so be it.

Compulsory purchase of annuities has therefore imposed large costs for little gain. It has deprived all of us of control over a sizable fraction of our income, requiring us to devote it to a particular purpose, purchase of a retirement annuity, in a particular way, by buying it from a government concern. It has inhibited competition in the sale of annuities and the development of retirement arrangements. It has given birth to a large bureaucracy that shows tendencies of growing by what it feeds on, of extending its scope from one area of our life to another. And all this, to avoid the danger that a few people might become charges on the public.

Chapter XII

The Alleviation
of Poverty

T HE EXTRAORDINARY ECONOMIC GROWTH experienced by Western countries during the past two centuries and the wide distribution of the benefits of free enterprise have enormously reduced
the extent of poverty in any absolute sense in the capitalistic
countries of the West. But poverty is in part a relative matter,
and even in these countries, there are clearly many people living
under conditions that the rest of us label as poverty.

One recourse, and in many ways the most desirable, is private
charity. It is noteworthy that the heyday of laissez-faire, the
middle and late nineteenth century in Britain and the United
States, saw an extraordinary proliferation of private eleemosynary organizations and institutions. One of the major costs of

the extension of governmental welfare activities has been the corresponding decline in private charitable activities.

It can be argued that private charity is insufficient because the benefits from it accrue to people other than those who make the gifts — again, a neighborhood effect. I am distressed by the sight of poverty; I am benefited by its alleviation; but I am benefited equally whether I or someone else pays for its alleviation; the benefits of other people's charity therefore partly accrue to me. To put it differently, we might all of us be willing to contribute to the relief of poverty, *provided* everyone else did. We might not be willing to contribute the same amount without such assurance. In small communities, public pressure can suffice to realize the proviso even with private charity. In the large impersonal communities that are increasingly coming to dominate our society, it is much more difficult for it to do so.

Suppose one accepts, as I do, this line of reasoning as justifying governmental action to alleviate poverty; to set, as it were, a floor under the standard of life of every person in the community. There remain the questions, how much and how. I see no way of deciding "how much" except in terms of the amount of taxes we — by which I mean the great bulk of us — are willing to impose on ourselves for the purpose. The question, "how," affords more room for speculation.

Two things seem clear. First, if the objective is to alleviate poverty, we should have a program directed at helping the poor. There is every reason to help the poor man who happens to be a farmer, not because he is a farmer but because he is poor. The program, that is, should be designed to help people as people not as members of particular occupational groups or age groups or wage-rate groups or labor organizations or industries. This is a defect of farm programs, general old-age benefits, minimum-wage laws, pro-union legislation, tariffs, licensing provisions of crafts or professions, and so on in seemingly endless profusion. Second, so far as possible the program should, while operating through the market, not distort the market or impede its functioning. This is a defect of price supports, minimum-wage laws, tariffs and the like.

The arrangement that recommends itself on purely mechani-

cal grounds is a negative income tax. We now have an exemption of $600 per person under the federal income tax (plus a
minimum 10 per cent flat deduction). If an individual receives
$100 taxable income, i.e., an income of $100 in excess of the
exemption and deductions, he pays a tax. Under the proposal, if
his taxable income minus $100, i.e., $100 less than the exemption
plus deductions, he would pay a negative tax, i.e., receive a
subsidy. If the rate of subsidy were, say, 50 per cent, he would
receive $50. If he had no income at all, and, for simplicity, no
deductions, and the rate were constant, he would receive $300.
He might receive more than this if he had deductions, for example, for medical expenses, so that his income less deductions,
was negative even before subtracting the exemption. The rates
of subsidy could, of course, be graduated just as the rates of tax
above the exemption are. In this way, it would be possible to set
a floor below which no man's net income (defined now to include the subsidy) could fall — in the simple example $300 per
person. The precise floor set would depend on what the community could afford.

The advantages of this arrangement are clear. It is directed
specifically at the problem of poverty. It gives help in the form
most useful to the individual, namely, cash. It is general and
could be substituted for the host of special measures now in
effect. It makes explicit the cost borne by society. It operates
outside the market. Like any other measures to alleviate poverty, it reduces the incentives of those helped to help themselves,
but it does not eliminate that incentive entirely, as a system of
supplementing incomes up to some fixed minimum would. An
extra dollar earned always means more money available for
expenditure.

No doubt there would be problems of administration, but
these seem to me a minor disadvantage, if they be a disadvantage at all. The system would fit directly into our current
income tax system and could be administered along with it.
The present tax system covers the bulk of income recipients
and the necessity of covering all would have the by-product of
improving the operation of the present income tax. More important, if enacted as a substitute for the present rag bag of

measures directed at the same end, the total administrative burden would surely be reduced.

A few brief calculations suggest also that this proposal could be far less costly in money, let alone in the degree of governmental intervention involved, than our present collection of welfare measures. Alternatively, these calculations can be regarded as showing how wasteful our present measures are, judged as measures for helping the poor.

In 1961, government amounted to something like $33 billion (federal, state, and local) on direct welfare payments and programs of all kinds : old age assistance, social security benefit payments, aid to dependent children, general assistance, farm price support programs, public housing, etc.[1] I have excluded veterans' benefits in making this calculation. I have also made no allowance for the direct and indirect costs of such measures as minimum-wage laws, tariffs, licensing provisions, and so on, or for the costs of public health activities, state and local expenditures on hospitals, mental institutions, and the like.

There are approximately 57 million consumer units (unattached individuals and families) in the United States. The 1961 expenditures of $33 billion would have financed outright cash grants of nearly $6,000 per consumer unit to the 10 per cent with the lowest incomes. Such grants would have raised their incomes above the average for all units in the United States. Alternatively, these expenditures would have financed grants of nearly $3,000 per consumer unit to the 20 per cent with the lowest incomes. Even if one went so far as that one-third whom New Dealers were fond of calling ill-fed, ill-housed, and ill-clothed, 1961 expenditures would have financed grants of nearly $2,000 per consumer unit, roughly the sum which, after allowing for the change in the level of prices, was the income which separated the lower one-third in the middle 1930's from the

[1] This figure is equal to government transfer payments ($31.1 billion) less veterans' benefits ($4.8 billion), both from the Department of Commerce national income accounts, plus federal expenditures on the agricultural program ($5.5 billion) plus federal expenditures on public housing and other aids to housing ($0.5 billion), both for year ending June 30, 1961 from Treasury accounts, plus a rough allowance of $0.7 billion to raise it to even billions and to allow for administrative costs of federal programs, omitted state and local programs, and miscellaneous items. My guess is that this figure is a substantial underestimate.

upper two-thirds. Today, fewer than one-eighth of consumer units have an income, adjusted for the change in the level of prices, as low as that of the lowest third in the middle 1930's.

Clearly, these are all far more extravagant programs than can be justified to "alleviate poverty" even by a rather generous interpretation of that term. A program which *supplemented* the incomes of the 20 per cent of the consumer units with the lowest incomes so as to raise them to the lowest income of the rest would cost less than half of what we are now spending.

The major disadvantage of the proposed negative income tax is its political implications. It establishes a system under which taxes are imposed on some to pay subsidies to others. And presumably, these others have a vote. There is always the danger that instead of being an arrangement under which the great majority tax themselves willingly to help an unfortunate minority, it will be converted into one under which a majority imposes taxes for its own benefit on an unwilling minority. Because this proposal makes the process so explicit, the danger is perhaps greater than with other measures. I see no solution to this problem except to rely on the self-restraint and good will of the electorate.

Writing about a corresponding problem — British old-age pensions — in 1914, Dicey said, "Surely a sensible and a benevolent man may well ask himself whether England as a whole will gain by enacting that the receipt of poor relief, in the shape of a pension, shall be consistent with the pensioner's retaining the right to join in the election of a Member of Parliament." [2]

The verdict of experience in Britain on Dicey's question must as yet be regarded as mixed. England did move to universal suffrage without the disfranchisement of either pensioners or other recipients of state aid. And there has been an enormous expansion of taxation of some for the benefit of others, which must surely be regarded as having retarded Britain's growth, and so may not even have benefited most of those who regard themselves as on the receiving end. But these measures have not destroyed, at least as yet, Britain's liberties or its predominantly capitalistic system. And, more important, there have been some

[2] A. V. Dicey, *Law and Public Opinion in England*, (2d ed., London: Macmillan, 1914), p. xxxv.

signs of a turning of the tide and of the exercise of self-restraint on the part of the electorate.

LIBERALISM AND EGALITARIANISM

The heart of the liberal philosophy is a belief in the dignity of the individual, in his freedom to make the most of his capacities and opportunities according to his own lights, subject only to the proviso that he not interfere with the freedom of other individuals to do the same. This implies a belief in the equality of men in one sense; in their inequality in another. Each man has an equal right to freedom. This is an important and fundamental right precisely because men are different, because one man will want to do different things with his freedom than another, and in the process can contribute more than another to the general culture of the society in which many men live.

The liberal will therefore distinguish sharply between equality of rights and equality of opportunity, on the one hand, and material equality or equality of outcome on the other. He may welcome the fact that a free society in fact tends toward greater material equality than any other yet tried. But he will regard this as a desirable by-product of a free society, not its major justification. He will welcome measures that promote both freedom and equality — such as measures to eliminate monopoly power and to improve the operation of the market. He will regard private charity directed at helping the less fortunate as an example of the proper use of freedom. And he may approve state action toward ameliorating poverty as a more effective way in which the great bulk of the community can achieve a common objective. He will do so with regret, however, at having to substitute compulsory for voluntary action.

The egalitarian will go this far, too. But he will want to go further. He will defend taking from some to give to others, not as a more effective means whereby the "some" can achieve an objective they want to achieve, but on grounds of "justice." At this point, equality comes sharply into conflict with freedom; one must choose. One cannot be both an egalitarian, in this sense, and a liberal.

Chapter XIII

Conclusion

IN THE 1920's and the 1930's, intellectuals in the United States were overwhelmingly persuaded that capitalism was a defective system inhibiting economic well-being and thereby freedom, and that the hope for the future lay in a greater measure of deliberate control by political authorities over economic affairs. The conversion of the intellectuals was not achieved by the example of any actual collectivist society, though it undoubtedly was much hastened by the establishment of a communist society in Russia and the glowing hopes placed in it. The conversion of the intellectuals was achieved by a comparison between the existing state of affairs, with all its injustices and defects, and a hypothetical state of affairs as it might be. The actual was compared with the ideal.

At the time, not much else was possible. True, mankind had

experienced many epochs of centralized control, of detailed intervention by the state into economic affairs. But there had been a revolution in politics, in science, and in technology. Surely, it was argued, we can do far better with a democratic political structure, modern tools, and modern science than was possible in earlier ages.

The attitudes of that time are still with us. There is still a tendency to regard any existing government intervention as desirable, to attribute all evils to the market, and to evaluate new proposals for government control in their ideal form, as they might work if run by able, disinterested men, free from the pressure of special interest groups. The proponents of limited government and free enterprise are still on the defensive.

Yet, conditions have changed. We now have several decades of experience with governmental intervention. It is no longer necessary to compare the market as it actually operates and government intervention as it ideally might operate. We can compare the actual with the actual.

If we do so, it is clear that the difference between the actual operation of the market and its ideal operation — great though it undoubtedly is — is as nothing compared to the difference between the actual effects of government intervention and their intended effects. Who can now see any great hope for the advancement of men's freedom and dignity in the massive tyranny and despotism that hold sway in Russia? Wrote Marx and Engels in *The Communist Manifesto*: "The proletarians have nothing to lose but their chains. They have a world to win." Who today can regard the chains of the proletarians in the Soviet Union as weaker than the chains of the proletarians in the United States, or Britain or France or Germany or any Western state?

Let us look closer to home. Which if any of the great "reforms" of past decades has achieved its objectives? Have the good intentions of the proponents of these reforms been realized?

Regulation of the railroads to protect the consumer quickly became an instrument whereby the railroads could protect themselves from the competition of newly emerging rivals — at the expense, of course, of the consumer.

An income tax initially enacted at low rates and later seized upon as a means to redistribute income in favor of the lower classes has become a facade, covering loopholes and special provisions that render rates that are highly graduated on paper largely ineffective. A flat rate of 23½ per cent on presently taxable income would yield as much revenue as the present rates graduated from 20 to 91 per cent. An income tax intended to reduce inequality and promote the diffusion of wealth has in practice fostered reinvestment of corporate earnings, thereby favoring the growth of large corporations, inhibiting the operation of the capital market, and discouraging the establishment of new enterprises.

Monetary reforms, intended to promote stability in economic activity and prices, exacerbated inflation during and after World War I and fostered a higher degree of instability thereafter than had ever been experienced before. The monetary authorities they established bear primary responsibility for converting a serious economic contraction into the catastrophe of the Great Depresson from 1929–33. A system established largely to prevent bank panics produced the most severe banking panic in American history.

An agricultural program intended to help impecunious farmers and to remove what were alleged to be basic dislocations in the organization of agriculture has become a national scandal that has wasted public funds, distorted the use of resources, riveted increasingly heavy and detailed controls on farmers, interfered seriously with United States foreign policy, and withal has done little to help the impecunious farmer.

A housing program intended to improve the housing conditions of the poor, to reduce juvenile delinquency, and to contribute to the removal of urban slums, has worsened the housing conditions of the poor, contributed to juvenile delinquency, and spread urban blight.

In the 1930's, "labor" was synonomous with "labor union" to the intellectual community; faith in the purity and virtue of labor unions was on a par with faith in home and motherhood. Extensive legislation was enacted to favor labor unions and to foster "fair" labor relation. Labor unions waxed in strength. By the 1950's, "labor union" was almost a dirty word; it was no longer synonomous with "labor," no longer automatically to be taken for granted as on the side of the angels.

Social security measures were enacted to make receipt of assistance a matter of right, to eliminate the need for direct relief and assistance. Millions now receive social security benefits. Yet the relief rolls grow and the sums spent on direct assistance mount.

The list can easily be lengthened: the silver purchase program of the 1930's, public power projects, foreign aid programs of the post-war years, F.C.C., urban redevelopment programs, the stockpiling program — these and many more have had effects very different and generally quite opposite from those intended.

There have been some exceptions. The expressways crisscrossing the country, magnificent dams spanning great rivers, orbiting satellites are all tributes to the capacity of government to command great resources. The school system, with all its defects and problems, with all the possibility of improvement through bringing into more effective play the forces of the market, has widened the opportunities available to American youth and contributed to the extension of freedom. It is a testament to the public-spirited efforts of the many tens of thousands who have served on local school boards and to the willingness of the public to bear heavy taxes for what they regarded as a public purpose. The Sherman antitrust laws, with all their problems of detailed administration, have by their very existence fostered competition. Public health measures have contributed to the reduction of infectious disease. Assistance measures have relieved suffering and distress. Local authorities have often provided facilities essential to the life of communities. Law and order have been maintained, though in many a large city the performance of even this elementary function of government has been far from satisfactory. As a citizen of Chicago, I speak feelingly.

If a balance be struck, there can be little doubt that the record is dismal. The greater part of the new ventures undertaken by government in the past few decades have failed to achieve their objectives. The United States has continued to progress; its citizens have become better fed, better clothed, better housed, and better transported; class and social distinctions have narrowed; minority groups have become less disadvantaged; popular culture has advanced by leaps and bounds. All this has been the product of the initiative and drive of individuals co-operating through the free market. Government measures have hampered not helped this development. We have been able to afford and surmount these measures only because of the extraordinary fecundity of the market. The invisible hand has been more potent for progress than the visible hand for retrogression.

Is it an accident that so many of the governmental reforms of recent decades have gone awry, that the bright hopes have turned to ashes? Is it simply because the programs are faulty in detail?

I believe the answer is clearly in the negative. The central defect of these measures is that they seek through government to force people to act against their own immediate interests in order to promote a supposedly general interest. They seek to resolve what is supposedly a conflict of interest, or a difference in view about interests, not by establishing a framework that will eliminate the conflict, or by persuading people to have different interests, but by forcing people to act against their own interest. They substitute the values of outsiders for the values of participants; either some telling others what is good for them, or the government taking from some to benefit others. These measures are therefore countered by one of the strongest and most creative forces known to man — the attempt by millions of individuals to promote their own interests, to live their lives by their own values. This is the major reason why the measures have so often had the opposite of the effects intended. It is also one of the major strengths of a free society and explains why governmental regulation does not strangle it.

The interests of which I speak are not simply narrow self-regarding interests. On the contrary, they include the whole range of values that men hold dear and for which they are willing to spend their fortunes and sacrifice their lives. The Germans who lost their lives opposing Adolf Hitler were pursuing their interests as they saw them. So also are the men and women who devote great effort and time to charitable, educational, and religious activities. Naturally, such interests are the major ones for few men. It is the virtue of a free society that it nonetheless permits these interests full scope and does not subordinate them to the narrow materialistic interests that dominate the bulk of mankind. That is why capitalist societies are less materialistic than collectivist societies.

Why is it, in light of the record, that the burden of proof still seems to rest on those of us who oppose new government programs and who seek to reduce the already unduly large role of government? Let Dicey answer: "The beneficial effect of State intervention, especially in the form of legislation, is direct, immediate, and, so to speak, visible, whilst its evil effects are gradual and indirect, and lie out of sight. . . . Nor . . . do most people keep in mind that State inspectors may be incompetent, careless, or even occasionally corrupt . . . ; few are those who realize the undeniable truth that State help kills self-help. Hence the majority of mankind must almost of necessity look with undue favor upon governmental intervention. This natural bias can be counteracted only by the existence, in a given society, . . . of a presumption or prejudice in favor of individual liberty, that is, of laissez-faire. The mere decline, therefore, of faith in self-help — and that such a decline has taken place is certain — is of itself sufficient to account for the growth of legislation tending towards socialism."[1]

The preservation and expansion of freedom are today threatened from two directions. The one threat is obvious and clear. It is the external threat coming from the evil men in the Kremlin who promise to bury us. The other threat is far more subtle. It is the internal threat coming from men of good intentions and good will who wish to reform us. Impatient with the slowness of persuasion and example to achieve the great social changes they envision, they are anxious to use the power of the state to achieve their ends and confident of their own ability to do so. Yet if they gained the power, they would fail to achieve their immediate aims and, in addition, would produce a collective state from which they would recoil in horror and of which they would be among the first victims. Concentrated power is not rendered harmless by the good intentions of those who create it.

The two threats unfortunately reinforce one another. Even if we avoid a nuclear holocaust, the threat from the Kremlin requires us to devote a sizable fraction of our resources to our

[1] A. V. Dicey, *op. cit.*, pp. 257-8.

military defense. The importance of government as a buyer of so much of our output, and the sole buyer of the output of many firms and industries, already concentrates a dangerous amount of economic power in the hands of the political authorities, changes the environment in which business operates and the criteria relevant for business success, and in these and other ways endangers a free market. This danger we cannot avoid. But we needlessly intensify it by continuing the present widespread governmental intervention in areas unrelated to the military defense of the nation and by undertaking ever new governmental programs — from medical care for the aged to lunar exploration.

As Adam Smith once said, "There is much ruin in a nation". Our basic structure of values and the interwoven network of free institutions will withstand much. I believe that we shall be able to preserve and extend freedom despite the size of the military programs and despite the economic powers already concentrated in Washington. But we shall be able to do so only if we awake to the threat that we face, only if we persuade our fellow men that free institutions offer a surer, if perhaps at times a slower, route to the ends they seek than the coercive power of the state. The glimmerings of change that are already apparent in the intellectual climate are a hopeful augury.

Index